Christopher Gist

David B. McCoy

Spare Change Press
Est. 1979

Christopher Gist, Second Edition © David B. McCoy, 2022.

Cover photo: Conkle's Hollow located within Hocking Hills State Park, Ohio.

Page one art:
Emerson's magazine and Putnam's monthly, Volume 5, NO 40, 1857.

The author would like to thank Mary Ann D'Aurelio and Dr. Rhonda Baughman for proofreading; Christian Wig for his advice concerning content and facts for the first edition; and Lannie Dietle for his assistance on this second edition.

Spare Change Press®
Massillon, OH 44646
sparechangepress79@gmail.com

Contents

Christopher Gist

Appendix I: Extracts from the *History of Cincinnati and the Territory of Ohio by* Adolphus E. Jones

Appendix II: Extracts from Chapter 3, *The Ohio by* Richard Elwell Banta

Appendix III: Christopher Gist Timeline

Before reading, it is recommended that one watches the first section of the following video on YouTube.

Once at YouTube, type in the search box:
"PBS The War That Made American Part 1"

INTRODUCTION TO FIRST EDITION

In American colonial history, no individual did more to bring about the early expansion west of the Appalachian Mountains into the Ohio Country than did Christopher Gist. In his fifty-four years, Christopher Gist was first a merchant and businessman in Baltimore, Maryland. He then became a Maryland Ranger, a surveyor, trapper, and trader. Between 1750-1752, Gist made two trans-Appalachian explorations for the Ohio Company of Virginia. In 1753 he accompanied George Washington to the French Fort, LeBoeuf (Waterford, PA), with a message demanding the French to leave the area claimed by the King of England. Shortly thereafter, he served as a scout for General Edward Braddock and was present at Braddock's defeat. In his last years, Gist served as a Deputy Agent to the Superintendent of Indian Affairs of the Southern Department. As pointed out by author Christian Wig, the "frontiersman [Christopher Gist] resembled Daniel Boone, Davy Crockett and all our frontier heroes rolled into one" (Wig, 2004).

INTRODUCTION TO SECOND EDITION

When I wrote the first edition of *Christopher Gist*, I was hoping to have it published by an ebook company in London called, History in an Hour. Here is how the publisher viewed his mission:

So slowly an idea formed in my mind of presenting history in its most digestible form ... Far from "dumbing down", HIAH would provide a way into history for people who may feel daunted by the mass and sheer length of new history titles that come out every year ... I knew there was a huge demand for history presented in such a way: quick reads for people on the go in this, our digital age.

That meant that some serious editing had to occur to keep under the 15,000 words limit.

Once I wrote and submitted my draft, HIAH was taken over by HarperCollins Press, London, and they decided to cease future publication of the series. I then published it through my publishing company, Spare Change Press, via Amazon. As it turned out, it has sold well.

As odd as this may sound, despite HarperPress publishing my short biography of George Washington before this book, I skimmed over Gist's role in keeping Washington alive in their journey to and from Ft. LeBoeuf. It truly is hard to imagine how our nation might be today without the presence of Washington. The highlights of that venture have also been addressed.

Finally, in addition to adding several more maps, I have included extracts from the *History of Cincinnati and the Territory of Ohio* by Adolphus E. Jones, and *The Ohio* by Richard Elwell Banta, to help in rounding out a description of Christopher Gist and the role he played in the development of settling this nation.

ONE

Christopher Gist was a frontiersman, surveyor, and accomplished explorer. His grandfather, Christopher Gist, was an immigrant from England. His wife, Edith Cromwell, was a distant relative of Oliver Cromwell. From 1653 to 1658, Cromwell served as lord protector of England, Wales, Scotland, and Ireland. Sometime before 1682 Christopher and Edith settled on the south side of the Patapsco River in Baltimore County, Maryland. Gist was a member of the Baltimore County grand jury in 1682, and one of the justices of the county in 1689.

Richard Gist, born in 1684 in Baltimore County, was the only child of Christopher Gist and Edith Cromwell. When a young man he was responsible for much of the surveying along the western shore of Maryland and became an extensive holder of land. Richard was a Baltimore County commissioner for a number of years and one of the seven commissioners appointed to lay out and oversee the building of Baltimore.

Richard Gist, and wife Zipporah Murray, had four sons and two daughters. Christopher, the eldest son, was born about 1705, and his early years were spent on the home plantation where he helped his father expand their mercantile business. It would be from his father that Christopher learned a great deal about furs, fur traders, and Indians. He also acquired from his father the skills needed to be a noted surveyor. Christopher would go on to survey and clear roads in Baltimore County, receiving an appointment as overseer of the roads in 1734.

It was during this time that Baltimore County created a type of militia known as the Maryland Rangers to protect citizens from possible Indian reprisals. As the name suggests, they ranged the countryside to protect any outlying settlers when there was trouble with the Indians. It was as a Ranger that Christopher became knowledgeable about Indian customs and the frontier of western Maryland and Pennsylvania. It was also his early training ground for the years he would later spend on the frontier.

When Christopher became thirty-seven, he opened his own fur trading business in Baltimore. He worked at the fur trading profession for several years, then disaster struck. His storehouse of furs was destroyed by fire, and he would spend the rest of his life repaying all the debts he incurred. By November 1745, his mounting debts forced him to sell his home "lying on the water with a good brick dwelling house, well furnished, a kitchen, stable, and a sundry of other outbuildings." Following this ill-fortune, he moved to a farm on the Yadkin River in northern North Carolina, a location that was out on the extreme frontier.

Little is known of the activities of Christopher and his family during this time. It is likely Christopher and his sons divided their time between farming, hunting, and collecting furs. Because of his merchandising background, he may have carried on trade with the Indians since they lived so near to the Great Indian Warpath (part of the network of trails in eastern North America developed and used by Native Americans for traveling and trading).

As mentioned, the one thing we do know about Christopher is that he was noted far and wide for his ability as a surveyor. It was for this reason he was hired by the Ohio

Company of Virginia in 1750. The Companies purpose was to extend British trade to the then far West and settle the country for the English Crown. Gist's ability as a surveyor is evidenced in the journals he would later record for the Ohio. His carefully detailed reports and observations throughout the twelve hundred miles he was called upon to explore are surprisingly accurate. The English and spelling used in his journals were much above those of the ordinary Virginian. His easy grasp of the elements of geography and mineralogy shows his education consisted of considerably more than a mere study of the fundamentals of surveying. Whether this education was gained in school or in experience we cannot be sure, but whichever the case, the results were excellent.

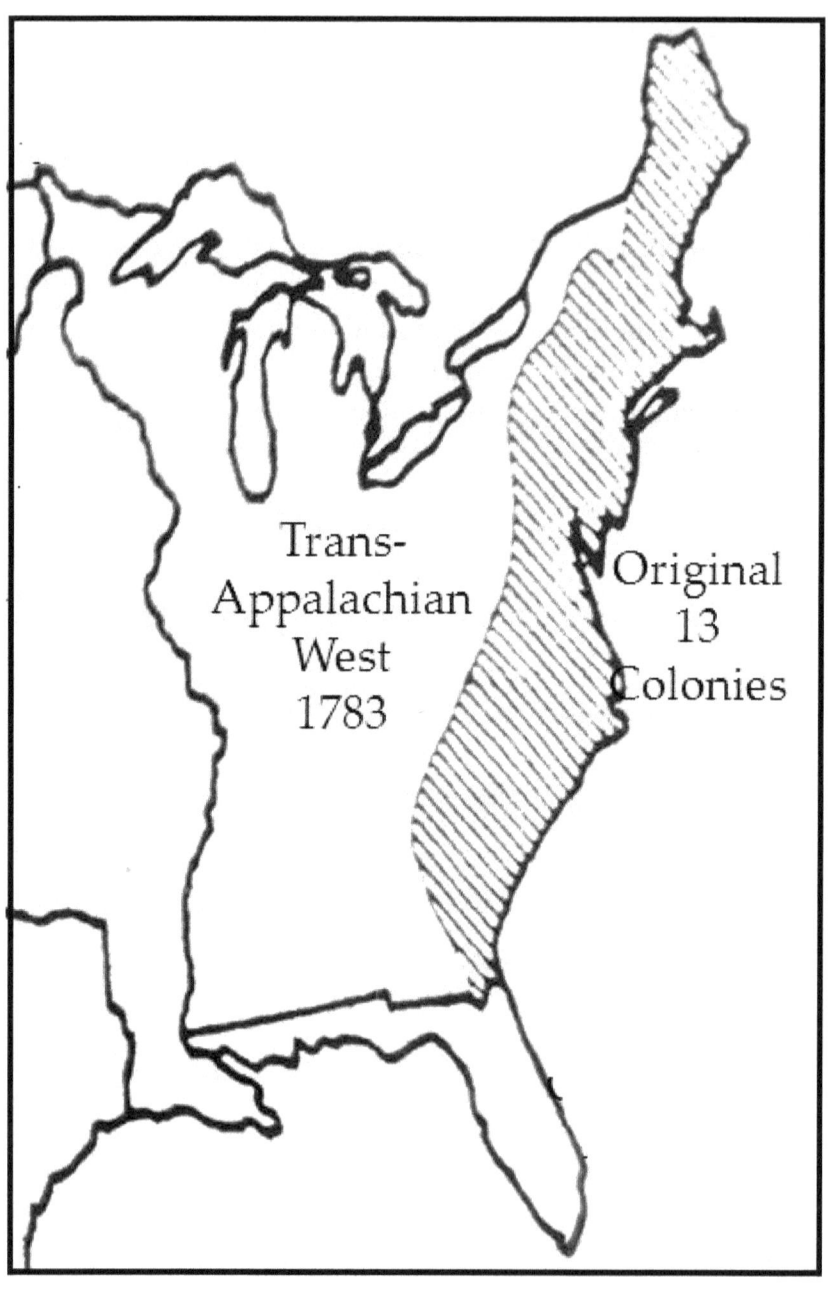

TWO

In the early part of the eighteenth century, the inhabitants of the trans-Appalachian region of North America remained much as it had been for the preceding centuries. Some were British trappers and backwoodsmen, and Frenchmen from Canada, but the principal occupants were Native Americans. As the British colonies became more populated and prosperous, their citizens began to look towards the rich lands across the Appalachian/Allegheny Mountains as providing new opportunities for settlement and economic growth.

The French, who claimed the entire watersheds of the Mississippi and St. Lawrence River, which included the Great Lakes and the Ohio River valley, became worried about British encroachments. To protect this region, they began to build a series of small forts: Presque Isle now (Erie, PA), LeBoeuf (Waterford, PA), and Venago (Franklin, PA). This was followed by the building of a much larger fort at the "Forks" where the Allegheny River merged with the Monongahela River to form the Ohio River. The British, meanwhile, built their own forts at Oswego, NY and Halifax, Nova Scotia and granted lands in the Ohio Valley to the Ohio Company.

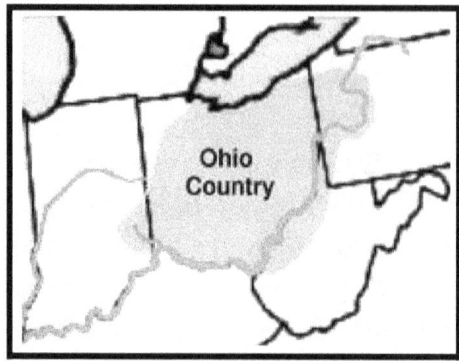

The Ohio Company, which had been formed by a number of influential gentlemen of England and Virginia, petitioned King George II in 1748 for five hundred thousand acres of land lying west of the Allegheny Mountains and in the Ohio Valley. In 1749, a charter was granted to the Company for two hundred thousand acres, on condition it settle a specified number of families and build a fort for their protection. Upon fulfilling this requirement, an additional three hundred thousand acres were to be made available for extending the proposed settlements. Governor Dinwiddie of Virginia and George Washington were later added as members of the Company, and Colonel Thomas Cresap was appointed field manager with headquarters at Wills Creek. (Wills Creek encompassed the area immediately surrounding the confluence of Wills Creek, a tributary of the North Branch of the Potomac River that flows through Maryland and Pennsylvania, and later was incorporated as Cumberland, Maryland. The area attained its name from European settlers, who referred to the land in honor of the Christian name they gave to a Shawnee Indian man, Will, who had considerable land claims around the creek during the first few decades of the eighteenth century.)

The British government supported the Ohio Company because it hoped the endeavor would interrupt French fur trading and provide a buffer state against rapidly expanding French settlements. During this time, beaver-felt tricorn hats came into fashion and there was a great demand for pelts. Where the Spanish discovered gold, the English and French discovered beaver pelts could be a great source of wealth.

In September 1749, the Company sent out various men, including Barney Curran, Hugh Parker—both traders who sold goods for the Company—to explore the land beyond the Allegheny Mountains and to make contact with the Indians. Also, Thomas Cresap was hired to open a road from Cumberland, Maryland, to the Monongahela River. But these men encountered opposition from both Indians and Pennsylvania traders and proved unsuccessful in their task. As a result, in 1750 the Company sent Christopher Gist on a similar mission. Ironically, Cresap at one time had lived in Baltimore where he was friends of the Gist family, and he was responsible for selecting Gist as an agent for the Company.

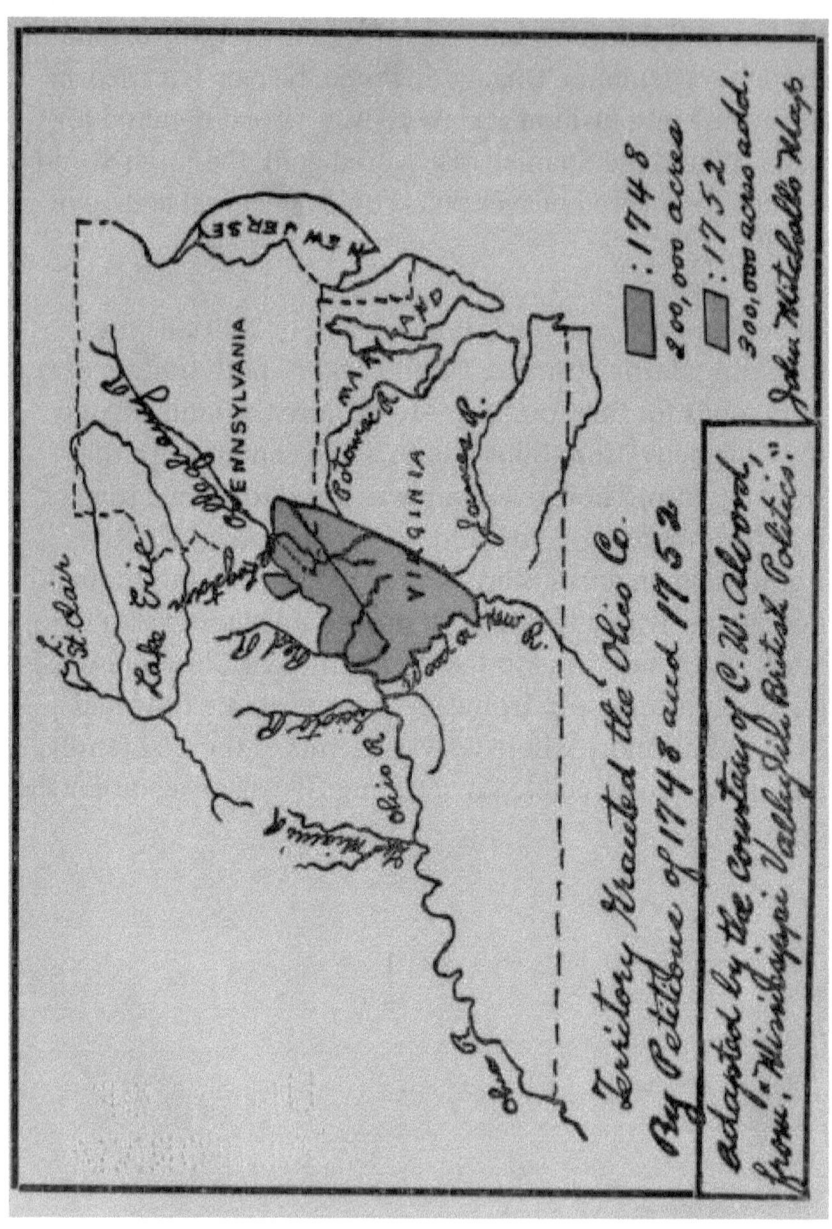

From, The Ohio Company a colonial corporation

THREE

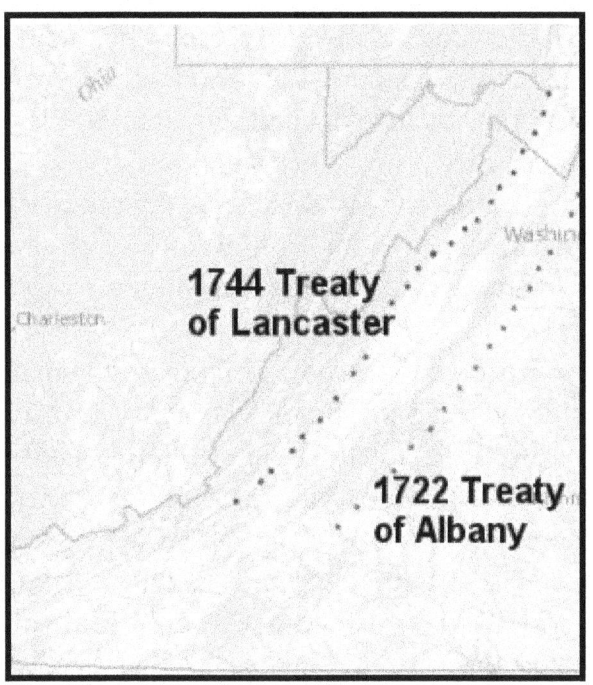

One of the most important background incidents in the history of the Ohio Company was the Treaty of Lancaster of 1744. This was one of the first tangible pieces of evidence on the part of English colonists in moving their beaver trapping into the Ohio country. This treaty was a milestone in Indian relations which served as a basis for much of the later negotiations and treaties with the Indians concerning their western land. Its chief importance lies in the fact it gave the English their first significant treaty claim to the Ohio region in their efforts to combat the claims of the French.

Nevertheless, the year 1744 was not the first occasion of an English attempt to settle disputes with the Indians regarding land to the west of the Alleghenies. In 1722, Governor Spotswood of Virginia had arrived at an agreement with the Indians, whereby the English were granted land as far west as the ridge of the Alleghenies, but no further. When the English began to advance beyond this line, the Native Americans protested these encroachments. To adjust these differences, a conference was called at Philadelphia in 1736 between the chiefs of the Six Nations and representatives of the Pennsylvania and Virginia governments.

While Pennsylvania appeared willing to grant concessions, Virginia did not. Virginia leaders claimed that the western territory in dispute belonged to her because of her charter and because of an earlier 1686 treaty. In this treaty, the Iroquois agreed to become the subjects of the British Crown and promised to give up their lands in return for protection. However, they apparently had never intended to actually turn over their lands to the English, and when colonists encroachment began to increase, the Iroquois leaders made their dissatisfaction known. For a time, it threatened to drive the Iroquois into open hostility toward the English and into close friendship with the French.

Faced with the possibility of alienating the Native Americans, representatives of Virginia, Maryland, and Pennsylvania, in conjunction with the chiefs of the Six Nations, agreed to the Lancaster Conference of 1744. The result of the treaty was the relinquishment on the part of the Iroquois of lands in Virginia and the acknowledgment of the right of the English King to this territory. In return, the Indians were given a payment of £400, partly in merchandise and partly in money. An additional assurance was given the Indians that they could have an open road through Virginia into the Catawba country in North Carolina. (Catawba Indians are often referred to as the Catawba Nation, a term that describes an eighteenth-century amalgamation of different peoples that included the Catawba Indians. Historically, the Indians who came to be called "Catawba" occupied the Catawba River Valley above and below the present-day North Carolina-South Carolina border.)

Confusion grew almost at once from this Lancaster Treaty. The Indians believed they had sold land only up to the headwaters of the rivers flowing westward into the Ohio; that they had successfully maintained claims in Virginia; that they had obtained a guarantee of an open trail to the Catawba country. Virginia, on the other hand, thought she had completely extinguished all claims of the Iroquois to land within that colony.

Due to the continued misunderstandings held by both sides, it was felt another gathering was necessary. Thus, one of Gist's jobs was to invite all tribes to a meeting at Logstown to be held in April 1752. In the minds of the English, it would serve as a way to confirm the Lancaster Treaty of 1744 in which, as the Virginians claimed, the Indians had acknowledged the right of the Colony of Virginia lands all the way to the Ohio River.

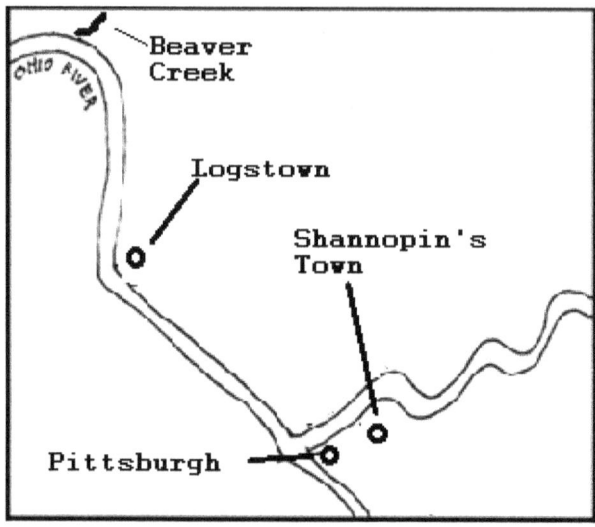

Logstown was located about eighteen miles from Shannopin's Town. It was just below the site of present-day Economy. The first description we have of Logstown is one made by Conrad Weiser in August, 1748. The town was first established by the Shawnee Indians in 1727-1730.

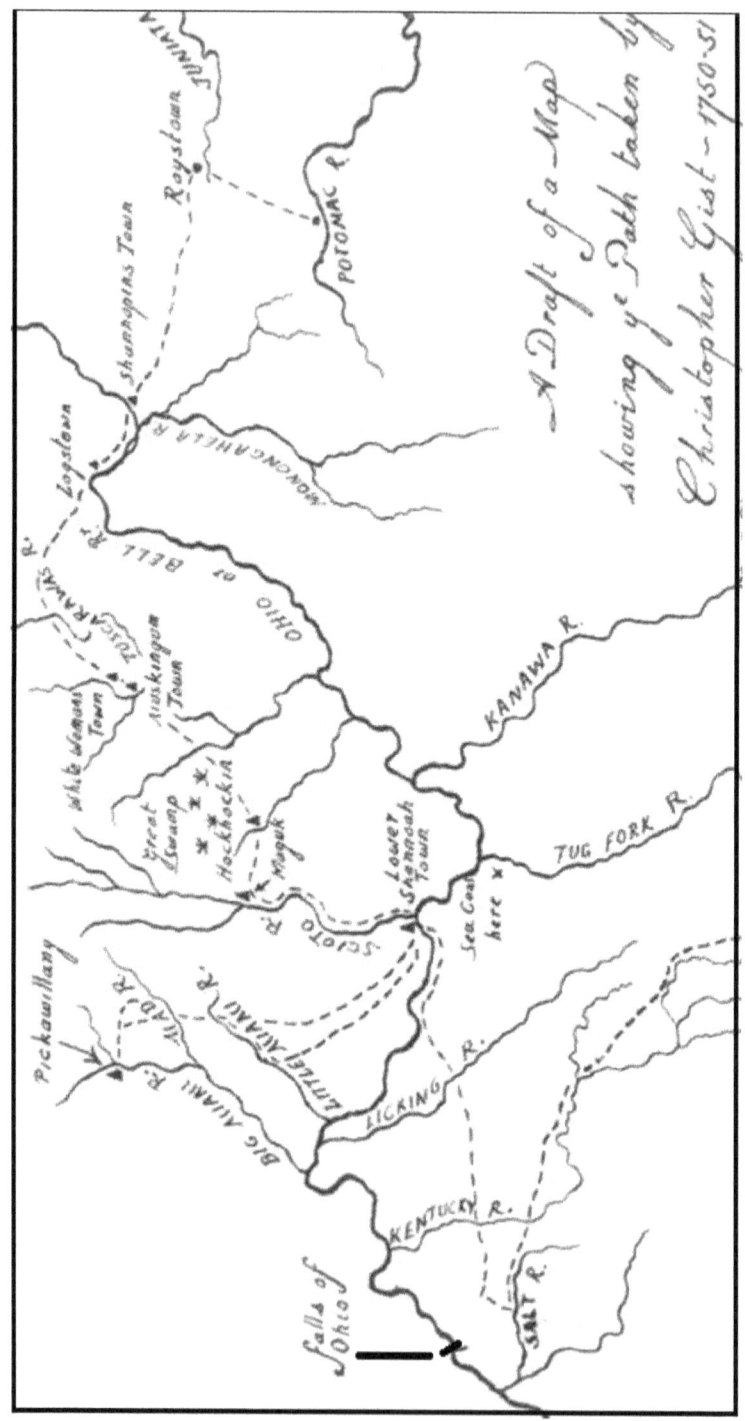

FOUR

On September 11, 1750, the committee of the Ohio Company gave Gist instructions to identify the passes through the mountains, to observe the courses of the rivers, and to journey as far west as the Great Falls of the Ohio. Particularly, Gist was to be on the lookout for fertile and accessible lands which would be suitable for settlement. He was instructted to observe the Indians that he encountered; note their relative strength and numbers, and the kind of items they bought and sold.

If Gist found a large area of fertile, level land which he thought would meet the wishes of the Company, he was to record a good description of its boundaries, measure it several ways, and determine its exact position so it could be easily found by following his description. In payment for his work, the Company agreed to give him a £150 sterling guarantee, as well as any additional sums which his services might deserve.

In accordance with his instructions, Gist set out upon his journey on October 31, 1750, from Old Town—Thomas Cresap's home on the Maryland side of the Potomac. From Old Town he traveled westward towards Shannopin's Town, a small Indian village of the Delawares at the Forks of the Ohio (present-day Pittsburgh).

[Henceforth, the italicized items are primarily the verbatim journal entries written by Gist. A few are those written by George Washington.]

Wednesday Oct 31 – Set out from Col. Thomas Cresap's at the old Town on Potomack River in Maryland, and went along an old Indian Path N 30 E about 11 Miles.

The trip from Old Town to Shannopin's Town took him twenty days. Thirteen days were spent in idleness due to sickness, snow, and rain. He noted that the country over which he passed, was for the most part, broken and stony, with an occasional good spot along the creeks, but not of sufficient size to be of use to the Company.

Tuesday 20 Wednesday 21 Thursday 22 and Friday 23 – The Land in general from Potomack to this Place is mean stony and broken, here and there good Spots upon the Creeks and Branches but no Body of it.

Gist spent four days at Shannopin's Town in an attempt to regain his health. While there he took the occasion to do a bit of exploring in the vicinity. He did not dare use his compass in public because it was dangerous to let the Indians realize that the true intent of the Ohio Company was to take their land. Consequently, Gist was forced to keep secret his real purpose and to pose as an envoy sent out by the Virginia government to reestablish peaceful relationships between the English and the Indians. He was able to do this by saying he was there to invite them to the meeting at Logstown Conference to be held in April 1752.

Tuesday 20 Wednesday 21 Thursday 22 and Friday 23 — I was unwell and stayed in this Town to recover myself; While I was here I took an Opportunity to set my Compass privately, & took the Distance across the River, for I understood it was dangerous to let a Compass be seen among these Indians: The River Ohio is 76 Poles wide at

Shannopin Town: There are about twenty Families in this Town.

* * *

To set his campus, Gist would first use the clock in combination with a magnetic compass to establish solar noon, when the sun crossed the celestial meridian (an imaginary line running due South to due North). He would then compare the difference in time between that place and a place whose solar time and longitude were already known (surveyors could use a chronometer, a specialized time piece that gave the time in a particular known location, or use published tables that gave position of the moon among the stars at specific times in a particular place, like Greenwich, England, and compare the difference in the moon's location), which made it possible to calculate the exact degree of longitude. With longitude established, he then recorded the angles stars made as they passed that specific line of longitude, called the meridian, allowing him to precisely establish the latitude of his position.

* * *

Gist set out on November 24 from Shannopin's Town, crossed the Ohio, and proceeded to Logstown, arriving there on the twenty-fifth. He found the land from Shannopin's Town to Logstown very fertile along the river, but the bottoms-lands were narrow. He noticed a short distance from the Ohio there was good level farming land, although it was covered with small white oaks.

Saturday 24 — Set out from Shannopin's Town, and swam our Horses across the River Ohio, & went down the River S 75 W 4 M, N 75 W 7 M W 2 M, all the Land from Shannopin's Town is good along the River, but the Bottoms not broad; At a Distance from the River good Land for Farming, covered with small white and red Oaks and tolerable level; fine Runs for Mills &c.[that could be used to turn waterwheels].

Gist found practically no one at Logstown except "a parcel of reprobate Indian traders, the chiefs of the Indians being out on a hunting." He seems not to have enjoyed his visit at this trading post. The inhabitants began to ask the nature of his business, and when he failed to give a prompt reply, they suspected him of scheming to take their lands—which was the Ohio Companies intent. In an attempt to avoid answering their questions, he tried to mislead them by ignoring their remarks.

Learning that George Croghan and Andrew Montour had recently passed that way, and knowing the high esteem in which the former was held by the Indians, Gist decided to pose as one of Croghan's friends.

George Croghan has been called the "prince of Pennsylvania traders." After immigrating to America in 1741 from Ireland, he became an Indian trader in 1744. For a number of years he traded privately and at the same time took part in Pennsylvania's Indian activities. In later years he became deputy Indian agent. Andrew Montour was the son of the famous half-breed Madame Montour. Montour became a very useful Indian interpreter. He was also very protective of Indian lands. Both men also knew the real reason Gist was sent out by the Ohio Company.

It quickly became apparent to Gist that if his real purpose was known, his life would be in danger. Not only did he claim the two men were his friends, he claimed he needed to catch up with Montour because he had a message from the government of Virginia for the Indians which needed to be translated. This partial fabrication served its purpose and made possible Gist's escape. In his own words the reason for his hasty departure was that "Tho I was unwell, I preferred the woods to such Company. . ."

Sunday Nov. 25 – Here I was informed that George Croghan & Andrew Montour who were sent upon an Embassy from Pensylvania to the Indians, were passed about a Week before me. The People in this Town, began to enquire my Business, and because I did not readily inform them, they began to suspect me, and said, I was come to settle the Indian's Lands and they knew I should never go Home again safe; I found this Discourse was like to be of ill Consequence to me, so I pretended to speak very slightingly of what they had said to me, and enquired for Croghan and Andrew Montour the Interpreter for Pensylvania, and told them I had a Message to deliver the Indians from the King, by Order of the President of Virginia, & for that Reason wanted to see M Montour: This made them all pretty easy (being afraid to interrupt the King's Message) and obtained me Quiet and Respect among them, otherwise I doubt not they woud have contrived some Evil against me — I imediately wrote to M Croghan, by one of the Trader's People.

From Logstown, Gist continued down the Ohio to Beaver Creek, so named for "The Beaver" (Tamaque), the king of the Delaware. At this point he encountered Barney Curran, an Ohio Company trader, and continued with him to the Indian town of Muskingum. (Muskingum was a Wyandot town located on the Tuscarawas River, a branch of the Muskingum River. It was located close to the present-day Coshocton.)

www.railsandtrails.com/Maps/OhioArch1914/OHArchAtlas1914-IndianTrails-100l.jpg
Once there, click to enlarge.

Gist, Curran, and eleven others continued through Columbiana County, traveling northwest to Hanoverton, Ohio. From there they moved westward, and slightly northward, to Bayard. Once in Carroll County, the party crossed a branch of the Tuscarawas River, known as Big Sandy Creek. On December 7, they stopped at the present town of Bolivar. By the ninth, they passed through the corner of Stark County into Tuscarawas County, reaching Muskingum on the fourteenth. Gist remained at Muskingum one month. On Christmas Day, he thought it would be a good thing to celebrate the day with some kind of religious ceremony using a few readings of the Church of England.

This service is believed to be the first Protestant religious service held within the present State of Ohio. Besides reflecting on Gist's faith, it shows the respect the Indians held for him.

Tuesday 25 — This being Christmass Day, I intended to read Prayers ... and Andrew Montour invited several of the well disposed Indians, who came freely ... I stood up and said, Gentlemen, I have no Design or Intention to give Offence to any particular Sectary or Religion, but as our King indulges Us all in a Liberty of Conscience and hinders none of You in the Exercise of your religious Worship, so it would be unjust in You, to endeavour to stop the Propagation of His; The Doctrine of Salvation Faith, and good Works, is what I only propose to treat of, as I find it extracted from the Homilies of the Church of England, which I then read them in the best Manner I coud, and after I had done the Interpreter told the Indians what I had read, and that it was the true Faith which the great King and His Church recomended to his Children: the Indians seemed well pleased, and came up to Me and returned Me their Thanks; and then invited Me to live among Them, and gave Me a Name in their Language Annosanah: the Interpreter told Me this was a Name of a good Man that had formerly lived among them, and their King said that must be always my Name, for which I returned them Thanks; but as to living among them I excused myself by saying I did not know whether the Governor woud give Me Leave, and if he did the French woud come and carry me away as they had done with other English Traders.

At Muskingum, Gist again met the mentioned Croghan who owned a trading house there. Gist found the town fairly evenly divided in its sympathy between the English and

French. During Gist's visit, news came of several English traders being taken by forty Frenchmen and twenty French Indians to a new fort the French were building on one of the branches of Lake Erie. Before leaving, Gist informed the Indians, through Montour, that the Ohio Company had gifts ready to distribute if they would come to the Forks of the Ohio in the spring to receive them. It was becoming clear that tensions between the French and the English were escalating.

Monday 14 — This Day George Croghan, by the Assistance of Andrew Montour, acquainted the King and Council of this Nation (by presenting them four Strings of Wampum) that the great King over the Water, their Roggony [Father] had sent under the Care of the Governor of Virginia, their Brother, a large Present of Goods which was now landed safe in Virginia, & the Governor had sent Me to invite Them to come and see Him, & partake of their Father's Charity to all his Children on the Branches of Ohio. In Answer to which one of the Chiefs stood up and said, That their King and all of Them thanked their Brother the Governor of Virginia for his Care, and Me for bringing them the News, but they coud not give Me an Answer untill they had a full or general Council of the several Nations of Indians which coud not be till next Spring: & so the King and Council shaking Hands with Us, We took our Leave.

www.railsandtrails.com/Maps/OhioArch1914/OHArchAtlas
1914-IndianTrails-100l.jpg
Once there, click to enlarge.

On January 15, 1751, Gist left Muskingum accompanied by Croghan, Montour, and their employees. Gist found the country from Logstown to Muskingum fairly good for farming and not badly broken up, but from Muskingum on, it was broken, although fertile. From Muskingum, he passed through Dresden, Clay Lick Station (6 miles east of Newark), Lancaster, near Circleville, and Shawnee Town before heading for the Twightwee town of Pickawillany.

www.railsandtrails.com/Maps/OhioArch1914/OHArchAtlas1914-IndianTrails-100l.jpg
Once there, click to enlarge.

(Pickawillany was located on the west bank of the Great Miami River at its junction with Laramie's creek, about two and one-half miles from the present town of Piqua.) En route he passed through the Indian towns of Delaware, Wyandot, and Shawnee, and in each instance invited the Indians to a conference at Logstown. He had planned to visit the Twightwees (Miami Indians), because Thomas Lee (a stockholder in the Company) had instructed him to find out the numbers and strength of certain Indians who lived west of the Ohio.

In his long entry of February 17, before his narrative of the Twightnwes, Gist provided a description of the land between the Little and Great Miami Rivers. He felt this was the best land for a future Ohio Company settlement. (However, when Gist delivered his journal, along with his maps and sketches, the Ohio Company committee rejected his recommendation. They felt the area was too far beyond Virginia's establish settlements, and it was too near the French military posts at Fort Detroit and Fort des Miamis.)

Sunday 17 —Crossed the little Miamee River, and altering our Course We went SW 25 M to the Big Miamee River, opposite the Twigtwee Town. All the way from the Shannoah Town to this Place ... is rich fine and level Land, well Timbered with large Walnut, Ash, Sugar Trees, Cherry Trees &c. It is well watered with a great Number of little Streams or Rivulets, and full of beautiful natural Meadows, covered with wild Rye, Blue Grass and clover, and abounds with Turkeys Deer, and Elks and most sorts of Game particularly Buffaloes, thirty or forty of which are frequently seen feeding in one meadow. In short, nothing but Cultivation to make it a most delightful Country — The Ohio [River] and all the large Branches are said to be full of fine Fish of several kinds particularly a Sort of Cat Fish of a prodigious size.

The Twightwees were considered English allies but it was Gist's duty to find out what influence the French might have with them and if the Ohio Company could safely plan to trade with them. In his journal, Gist explained the political setup of the Miamis and told of their great influence among neighboring tribes. He showed the characteristic mid-eighteenth-century lack of knowledge of American geography, however, when he surmised that the Twightwees might have great influence in the West, even possibly across the entire continent.

Sunday 17 – The Twigtwees are a very numerous People consisting of many different Tribes under the same Form of Government. Each tribe has a particular Chief or King, one of which is chosen indifferently out of any Tribe to rule the whole Nation, and is vested with greater Authorities than any of the others — They are accounted the most powerful People to the Westward of the English Settlements, & much superior to the six Nations with whom they are now in Amity: their Strength and Numbers are not thoroughly known, as they have but lately traded with the English, and indeed have very little Trade among them: they deal in much the same Comodities with the Northern Indians. There are other Nations or Tribes still further to the Westward daily coming in to them, & 'tis thought their Power and Interest reaches to the Westward of the Mississippi, if not across the Continent.

On February 17, Montour gave the standard speech he delivered to each tribe, this time stressing the need of clearing the French from the channels of trade. From February 20-22 more councils were held, often with additional foreign tribes. A considerable disorder was caused the next day by a reported invasion of the French, but it turned out to be only four French Indian envoys who were attempting to swing the Twightwees to a French alliance. They were not successful, however, for the Twightwee chiefs were able to point to the fact that even these French Indians were often at odds with the French Government. The result was an English alliance stronger than before. On the first day of March, the Twightwees declared they would be glad to come to Logstown to receive the Ohio Company's gifts.

Saturday 23 — In the Afternoon there was an Alarm in the Town which caused a great Confusion and running about among the Indians, upon enquiring into the Reason of this Stir, they told Us that it was occasioned by six Indians that came to war against Them, from the Southward : three of them Cutaways, and three Shanaws (these were some of the Shanaws who had formerly deserted from the other Part of the Nation, and now live to the Southward) Towards Night there was a report spread in Town that four Indians, and four hundred French, were on their March and just by the Town : But soon after the Messenger who brought this News said, there were only four French Indians coming to Council.

Sunday 24 — This Morning the four French Indians came into Town and were kindly received by the Town Indians; they marched in under French Colours, and were conducted into the long House, and after they had been in about a Quarter of an Hour, the Council sat, and We were sent for that We might hear what the French had to say to them — The Pyankeshee King (who was at that Time the principal Man, and Comander in Chief of the Twigtwees) said. He woud have the English Colours set up in this Council as well as the French, to which We answered he might do as he thought fit. After We were seated right opposite to the French Embassadors, One of Them said, He had a Present to make Them, so a Place was prepared (as they had before done for our Present) between Them and Us, and then their Speaker stood up, and layed His hands upon two small Caggs of Brandy that held about seven Quarts each, and a Roll of Tobacco of about ten Pounds Weight, then taking two strings of Wampum in his Hand, He said, "What he had to deliver Them was "from their Father (meaning the French King) and he desired they woud hear what he was about to say to Them; then he layed them two Strings of Wampum down upon the Caggs, and taking up four other Strings of black and white Wampum, he said, "that their Father remembring his Children, had sent them two Caggs of Milk, and some Tobacco, and that he now had made a clear Road for them, to come and see Him and his Officers; and pressed them very much to come ; then he took another String of Wampum in his Hand, and said, "their Father now woud forget all littie Differences that had been between Them, and desired Them not to be of two Minds, but to let Him know their Minds freely, for He woud send for Them no more — To which the Pyankeshee King replyed, "it was true their Father had sent for them several Times, and said the Road was clear, but He understood it was made foul & bloody, and by Them— We (said He) have cleared a Road for our Brothers the English, and your Fathers have made it bad, and have taken some of our Brothers Prisoners, Which We look upon as clone to Us, and he turned short about and went out of Council — After the French Embassador had delivered his Message He went into one of the private Houses and endeavoured much to prevail on some Indians, and was seen to cry and lament (as he said for the Loss of that Nation).

Tuesday 26 — The Twigtwees delivered the following Answer to the four Indians sent by the French — The Captain of the Warriors stood up and taking some Strings of black and white Wampum in his Hand he spoke with a fierce Tone and very warlike Air — Brothers the Ottaways, You are always differing with the French Yourselves, and yet You listen to what they say, but We will let You know by these four Strings of Wampum, that We will not hear any Thing they say to Us, nor do any Thing they bid Us.

Friday March 1 — We received the following Speech from the Twigtwees the Speaker stood up and addressing himself as to the Governor of Pensylvania with two Strings of Wampum in his Hand, He said — "Brothers our Hearts are glad that You have taken Notice of Us, and surely Brothers We hope that You will order a Smith to settle here to mend our Guns and Hatchets, Your Kindness makes Us so bold to ask this Request. You told Us our Friendship should last as long, and be as the greatest Mountain, We have considered well, and all our great Kings & Warriors are come to a Resolution never to give Heed to what the French say to Us, but always to hear & believe what You our Brothers say to Us — Brothers We are obliged to You for your kind Invitation to receive a Present at the Loggs Town.

On the next day, Gist, Croghan and the rest of the group started out again, but parted Company: Croghan headed for Hockhockin (Lancaster, Ohio), and Gist for Lower Shawnee Town (at the mouth of the Scioto River and modern-day Portsmouth, Ohio), a place he had visited on his way to Pickawillany. As the French Indians had threatened the travelers at Pickawillany, Gist feared they might be lying in wait for him on the return journey. Because he was alone, except for his servant, he did not follow the trail but went southwest along the Little Miami River. Along this route he found fertile land and great, beautiful meadows with hardly a bush in sight. On the eighth, he arrived at Shawnee Town, with no particular event of note having taken place on his journey.

Sunday 3 – I left the Path, and went to the South Westward down the little Miamee River or Creek, where I had fine traveling thro rich Land and beautiful Meadows, in which I coud sometimes see forty or fifty Buffaloes feeding at once— The little Miamee River or Creek continued to run thro the Middle of a fine Meadow, about a Mile wide very clear like an old Field, and not a Bush in it, I coud see the Buffaloes in it above two Miles off : I travelled this Day about 30 M[iles].

The inhabitants of Shawnee Town, both Indian and white, came out to meet him upon his return. A salute of about one hundred fifty guns was fired and subsequently a celebration was held in his honor. The next day he talked with a Mingo chief whom he had missed on his first visit because the chief had been down to the Falls of the Ohio. Gist extended an invitation to come to Logstown with the promise of gifts. The chief informed him of a French Indian party hunting near the Falls and suggested Gist refrain from going down in that direction as those Indians would surely take him prisoner and carry him to the French. But because of his desire to see the Falls, as well as to observe the country on the east side of the Ohio, he decided to venture as far as possible. [The Falls of the Ohio was one of the few unnavigable sections on the Ohio's 981-mile course. It's called the Falls the Ohio because the water falls two and a half feet and spans two and a half miles. It was a natural stopping point for all who came by river.]

Friday 8 — Travelled about 30 M, and arrived at Night at the Shawnee Town — All the Indians, as well as the white Men came out to welcome my Return to their Town, being very glad that all Things were rightly settled in the Miamee Country, they fired upwards of 150 Guns in the Town, and made an Entertainment in Honour of the late Peace with the western Indians — In my Return from the Twigtwee to the Shawnee Town, I did not keep an exact Account of Course or Distance ; for as the Land thereabouts was every where much the same, and the Situation of the Country was sufficiently described in my Journey to the Twigtwee Town, [The Land about the Mouth of Sciodoe Creek is rich but broken fine Bottoms upon the River & Creek].

Saturday March 9 — In the Shawnee Town, I met with one of the Mingoe Chiefs, who had been down at the Falls of Ohio, so that We did not see Him as We went up; I informed Him of the King's Present, and the Invitation down to

Virginia — He told that there was a Party of French Indians hunting at the Falls, and if I went there they would certainly kill Me or carry Me away Prisoner to the French; For it is certain they would not let Me pass: However as I had a great Inclination to see the Falls, and the Land on the E Side the Ohio, I resolved to venture as far as possible.

On March 13, Gist was on his way from Shawnee Town to the Falls when he met Hugh Crawford who had for him two teeth of a mammoth beast. These bones had been taken from one of the salt licks a short distance above the Falls. The rib bones were eleven feet long and the skull bone over six feet in width; several teeth were found that were about five inches long. The tooth Gist selected for the Ohio Company weighed over four pounds.

Wednesday 13 — We set out S 45 W, down the said River on the SE Side 8 M, then S 10 M, here I met two Men belonging to Robert Smith at whose House I lodged on this Side the Miamee River, and one Hugh Crawford, the said Robert Smith had given Me an Order upon these Men, for two of the Teeth of a large Beast, which they were bringing from towards the Falls of Ohio, one of which I brought in and delivered to the Ohio Company — Robert Smith informed Me that about seven Years ago these Teeth and Bones of three large Beasts (one of which was somewhat smaller than the other two) were found in a salt Lick or Spring upon a small Creek which runs into the S Side of the Ohio, about 15 M, below the Mouth of the great Miamee River, and 20 above the Falls of Ohio — He assured Me that the Rib Bones of the largest of these Beasts were eleven Feet long, and the Skull Bone six feet wide, across the Forehead, & the other Bones in Proportion; and that there were several Teeth there, some of which he called Horns, and said they were up- wards of five Feet long, and as much as a Man coud well carry: that he had hid one in a Branch at some Distance from the Place, lest the French Indians shoud carry it away — The Tooth which I brought in for the Ohio Company, was a Jaw Tooth of better than four Pounds Weight; it appeared to be the furthest Tooth in the Jaw, and looked like fine Ivory when the outside was scraped off.

Upon arriving within fifteen miles of the Great Falls, Gist found a number of signs of Indians. He wanted to continue but his sense of duty to the Company prevailed, so he turned southward. He headed for the Kentucky River, reaching it at about the site of present-day Frankfort KY. At various points along his route he observed extensive meadows. Near the mouth of Red River (central Kentucky) he found some stones which he thought might be of value, therefore he took some for the Company as samples. A short distance farther on he found some coal and brought some of it along, too. Because of the rough country he encountered, he found his progress slowed and was often short of food for both himself and his horses. From March 20 to May 7 he encountered constant difficulties. He lost several horses due to falls and similar trouble. When the route was not steep, he ran into thickets—and more likely than not he encountered both. To his relief he reached the extreme western settlement of Richard Hall's, located in what is Montgomery County, OH, on May 13.

Monday 18 – I was now much troubled that I could not comply with my Instructions, & was once resolved to leaye the Boy and Horses, and to go privately on Foot to view the Falls; but the Boy being a poor Hunter, was afraid he woud starve if I was long from him, and there was also great Danger lest the French Indians shoud come upon our Horses Tracts, or hear their Bells, and as I had seen good Land enough, I thought perhaps I might be blamed for venturing so far, in such dangerous Times, so I concluded not to go to the Falls ; but travell'd away to the Southward till We were over the [Kentucky] River — The Falls of Ohio by the best Information I coud get [probably at Shawnee Town]are not very steep, on the SE Side there is a Bar of Land at some Distance from the Shore, the Water between the Bar and the Shore is not above 3 feet deep, and the Stream moderately strong, the Indians frequently pass safely in their Canoes thro this Passage, but are obliged to take great Care as they go down lest the Current which is much the strongest on the NW Side shoud draw them that Way; which woud be very dangerous as the Water on that Side runs with great Rapidity over several Ledges of Rocks; the Water below the Falls they say is about six Fathoms deep, and the River continues without any Obstructions till it empties itself into the Missisippi which is accounted upwards of 400 M[iles].

Sunday 14 — As Food was very scarce in these barren Mountains, We were obliged to move for fresh Feeding for our Horses, so We went on E 5 M then N 20 W 6 M, to a Creek where We got something better Feeding for our Horses, in climbing up the Clifts and Rocks this Day two of our Horses fell down, and were pretty much hurt, and a Paroquete, which I had got from the Indians ... In the Afternoon I left the Horses, and went a little Way down the Creek, and found such a Precipice and such Laurel Thickets as We coud not pass, and the Horses were not able to go up the Mountain till they had rested a Day or two.

While resting at the home of Rich Hall, he wrote a letter to Thomas Lee and the Ohio Company informing them that he would be with them on June 15. Hall was one of "the farthest settlers to the westward upon the New River" (Gist). Upon leaving Hall's place he journeyed to his own home only to discover his family had been driven to the Roanoke River* by Indian raids.

Friday 17 — Set out SW 3 M then S 9 M, to the dividing Line between Carolina and Virginia, where I stayed all Night, the Land from Rich Hall's to this Place is broken.

Saturday 18 — Set out S 20, M to my own House on the Yadkin River, when I came there I found all my Family gone, for the Indians had killed five People in the Winter near that Place, which frightened my Wife and Family away to Roanoke about 35 M nearer in among the Inhabitants, which I was informed of by an old Man I met near the Place.

Sunday 19 — Set out for Roanoke, and as We had now a Path, We got there the same Night where I found all my Family well.

This completed Christopher Gist's first journey.

(*First called Big Lick, after a large outcropping of salt that drew the wildlife to the site near the Roanoke River. In 1882, Big Lick became the town of Roanoke.)

Wampum belts consist of carefully placed strings of knotted wampum beads, which are made from quahog clam, whelk, or cowrie shells.

The weaving of wampum belts is a sort of writing by means of belts of colored beads, in which the various designs of beads denoted different ideas according to a definitely accepted system, which could be read by anyone acquainted with wampum language, irrespective of what the spoken language is. Records and treaties are kept in this manner, and individuals could write letters to one another in this way. [William James Sidis, 1935.]

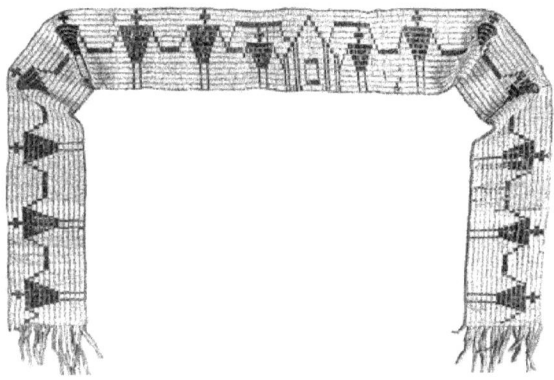

George Washington Belt

A.k.a: The 1794 Canandaigua Treaty belt. This belt is 6 feet long and composed of thirteen figures holding hands connected to two figures and a house. The 13 figures represent the 13 States of the newly formed United States of America. The two figures and the house symbolize the Iroquois Confederacy. President George Washington had this belt made to ratify the treaty with the Iroquois Confederacy to end the quarrels between the U.S. and the Iroquois. Each of the figures are linked to form a chain of friendship and peace, that will last forever.

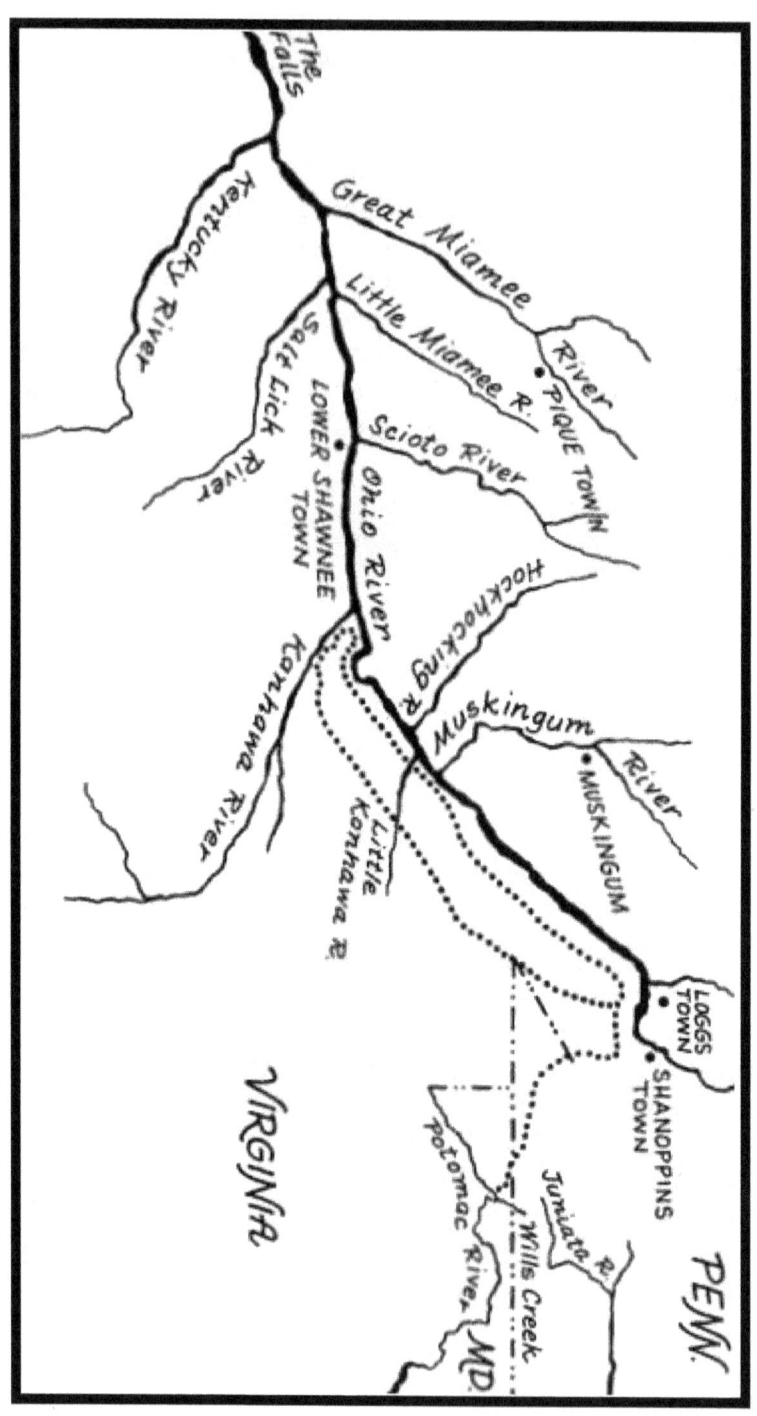

FIVE

A portrait of Gist was never made, but it is known that he was taller than average, husky, and of somewhat dark complexion. If he physically resembled his son, Nathaniel, then he was about six feet, two inches tall, and weighed about two hundred pounds. Throughout his life he was described as being a strong man capable of enduring great physical hardships.

Despite living most of his life away from civilization, he was not a "rough" man. He was unusual in that he could be as much at home in the lively political, cultural, and educational center of Williamsburg as on the frontier. He easily socialized with Indians, other woodsmen, and with the likes of George Washington and Lord Fairfax.

Few Englishmen had more success in dealing with Indians than Gist. The fact that he engaged in trading, negotiating, and obtaining land from Native Americans, and remained on peaceful terms, attests to his diplomatic skills.

However, Gist could be cunning and crafty. Whether he was working some kind of psychology on the Indians, or driving a clever bargain in purchasing supplies from whites, he remained a tough man in being able to get the best deal or agreement. Deal making may have been a strength, but the actual operations of a business proved a weakness.

* * *

After a brief visit with his family, Gist went to Williamsburg where he made his report and presented his journal to the

Ohio Company officers. He also decided that it would be best to move his family to Virginia where they would be safe from Indian attacks.

After reading Gist's journal, the Company noted that he had confined most of his observations to the north side of the Ohio. Because the area was too far beyond Virginia's establish settlements, and it was too near the French military posts at Fort Detroit and Fort des Miamis, it was decided to send him back, but this time to observe and examine lands on the south side of the Ohio. Gist's new instructions, dated July 16, 1751, ordered him to Thomas Cresap's place at Old Town and to secure as many of the Company's horses as he should deem necessary. Once supplied and staffed, he was to search for the shortest route from the Ohio Company's storehouse at Wills Creek to a point on Monongahela where goods and animals could be loaded onto boats.

He was to journey down the Ohio River until he came to the Big Kanawha, then to ascend that river as far as he could, all the while searching for good land to be settled. While not displeased with his first report, on this expedition he was asked to keep a more detailed journal, noting not only every fragment of good land, no matter how small, but to describe both value and vegetation. He was also to notice the length, breadth, and depth of all the streams flowing into the Ohio.

Gist set out from the Company's storehouse at Wills Creek on November 4, 1751. This time he was accompanied by his son, Nathaniel. From the Ohio Company's storehouse they crossed the Potomac River, then moved west about four miles through a gap in the Allegheny Mountains near the southwest fork of the Potomac. Though the mountains were high, at first he thought it was the best road to the Monongahela River.

Monday 4 – This Gap is the nearest to Potomack River of any in the Allegany Mountains, and is accounted one of the best, tho the Mountain is very high, The Ascent is no where very steep but rises gradually near 6 M, it is now very full of old Trees & Stones, but with some Pains might be made a good Waggon Road, this Gap is directly in the Way to Mohongaly, & several Miles nearer than that the Traders commonly pass thro, and a much better Way.

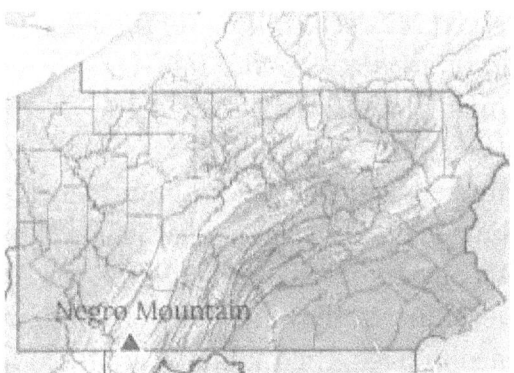
Officials in Maryland have removed several road signs pointing to 'Negro Mountain' over concerns about racial insensitivity in the name.

After passing over three successive mountain ranges west of Cumberland, then south to Little Meadow Run (stream) near Salisbury, PA, they climbed over Negro Mountain, and crossed the upper Youghiogheny River to camp near Gabrielle's Run in Fayette County, PA. (Negro Mountain or Cresap Mountain is a long ridge of the Allegheny Mountains in the eastern United States, stretching 30-mile (48 km) from Deep Creek Lake in Maryland north to the Casselman River in Pennsylvania. The summit, Mount Davis, is the highest point (3,213 feet) in Pennsylvania.) On November 24, they moved west, then south, then west again until they came to a small Hunting Town of the Delaware Indians. There they bought some corn and invited the Delaware "to the treaty at the Logstown, the full moon in May..." the Indians seemed friendly enough, but Gist learned afterwards they talked of causing him harm.

Sunday 24 — Set out W 2 M then S 45 W 6 M over the S Fork and encamp'd on the SW Side about 1 M from a small Hunting Town of the Delawares from whom I bought some Corn — I invited these Indians to the Treaty at the Loggs Town, the full Moon in May, as Col° Patton had desired Me; they treated Me very civilly, but after I went from that Place my Man informed Me that they threatened to take away our Guns and not let Us travel.

They next climbed over Briery Mountains, entered the Great Meadows (11 miles east of what is now Uniontown, PA), and then passed over Laurel Hill, the last Allegheny range. On December 7, they arrived at an Indian camp where Nemacolin lived, the Indian who later aided Cresap in marking out the Ohio Company road. Gist invited Nemacolin to Logstown the same as he had the other Indians. By the ninth, they reached the Monongahela at about six miles upstream from the present site of Brownsville. Six days later they started out again, crossing to the west side of the Monongahela. After spending considerable time exploring the surrounding country, he stopped at a camp upon Licking Creek belonging to an Indian named Oppaymolleah. Here Gist saw an Indian named Joshua with whom he had been acquainted with for several years. As with other Indians, Joshua wondered why they were traveling so far into the woods. (Certainly, it was not to just trade with the Indians.)

From December 21 to January 19, 1752, little progress was made because Gist's son was suffering from frostbitten feet. While exploring, Gist found some rocks with yellow-colored veins running through them. He took a sample of this for the Company, as he thought it might be a precious metal.

Thursday 13 — In the Place from whence it removed (a Piece of Land about 100 Yards square & about 10 Feet deep from the Surface had slipped down a steep Hill) was a large Quarry of Rocks, in the Sides of which were Veins of several Colours, particularly one of a deep yellow, about 3 Feet from the Bottom, in which were other small Veins some white, some a greenish Kind of Copperas : A Sample of which I brought in to the Ohio Company in a small Leather Bag N° 1 — Not very far from this Place We found another large Piece of Earth, which had slipped down in the same Manner — Not far from here We encamped in the Fork of a Creek.

On one rock he chiseled in large letters:

THE OHIO COMPANY
FEB 1751*
BY CHRISTOPHER GIST

[*In accordance with a 1750 act of Parliament, England and its colonies changed to the Gregorian calendar in 1752. This marked a switch from March 25 to January 1 as the first day of the year. Because Gist was on the frontier, he did not know, or forgot, about the change. The whereabout of the rock are unknown.]

From this point Gist continued his travels, running into no particular incidents of importance. He spent much of his time in lateral exploration rather than moving forward with any great speed. He went down the Ohio as far as the Big Kanawha and then turned homeward. Around the Kanawha the land was especially suitable for the Company's needs. By March 12, he was back at the Monongahela, and thereafter the Potomac. He did not follow quite the same route home from the Monongahela he had followed going but, instead, went more to the east, and in doing so, found a better way to travel.

Sunday 8. — We went out to search the Land which We found very good for near 15 M up this Creek from the Mouth of it, the Bottoms above a Mile wide & some Meadows — We found an old Indian Road up this Creek. Thursday 12 — I set out for Monongahela crossed it upon a Raft of Logs from whence I made the best of my Way to Potomac — I did not keep exactly my old Tract but went more to the Eastward & found a much nearer Way Home : and am of Opinion the Company may have a tolerable good Road from Wills Creek to the upper Fork of Monongahela, from whence the River is navigable all the Way to the Ohio for large flat bottomed Boats — The Road will be a little to the Southward of West, and the Distance to the Fork of Monongahela about 70 M[iles].

It was at this point, Gist met an Indian who spoke good English, and said their great Delaware chiefs, the "Beaver" and Captain Oppaymolleah desired to know where the Indians' land lay, for the French claimed all the land on one side of the River Ohio and the English on the other side.

Thursday 12 – I very well remembered that Oppaymolleah had asked me such a Question, and that I was at a Loss to answer Him as I now also was : But after some Consideration my Friend said I, " We are all one King's People and the different Colour of our Skins makes no Difference in the King's Subjects ; You are his People as well as We, if you will take Land & pay the King's Rights You will have the same Privileges as the White People have, and to hunt You have Liberty everywhere so that You don't kill the White Peoples Cattle & Hogs — To this the Indian said, that I must stay at that Place two Days and then he would come & see Me again, He then went away, and at the two Days End returned as he promised, and looking very pleasant said He would stay with Me all Night, after He had been with Me some Time He said that the great Men bid Him tell Me I was very safe that I might come and live upon that River where I pleased — that I had answered Them very true for We were all one King's People sure enough & for his Part he would come to see Me at Wills Creek in a Month.

Gist arrived at the Ohio Company storehouse at Wills Creek on March 29. His second journey, while historically not as important as his first, was much more to the liking of the Company. As noted, the Company decided to send Gist back, but this time to observe and examine lands on the south side of the Ohio. Also, he was asked to keep a more detailed journal, noting not only every fragment of good land, but to describe both value and vegetation. He was also to notice the length, breadth, and depth of all the streams flowing into the Ohio.

Unquestionably, Gist's journal was the best description of West Virginia, Ohio, western Maryland and western Pennsylvanian up to that time. It was accurate and complete. And accompanying the manuscript was a map of the region which greatly added to the value of his work.

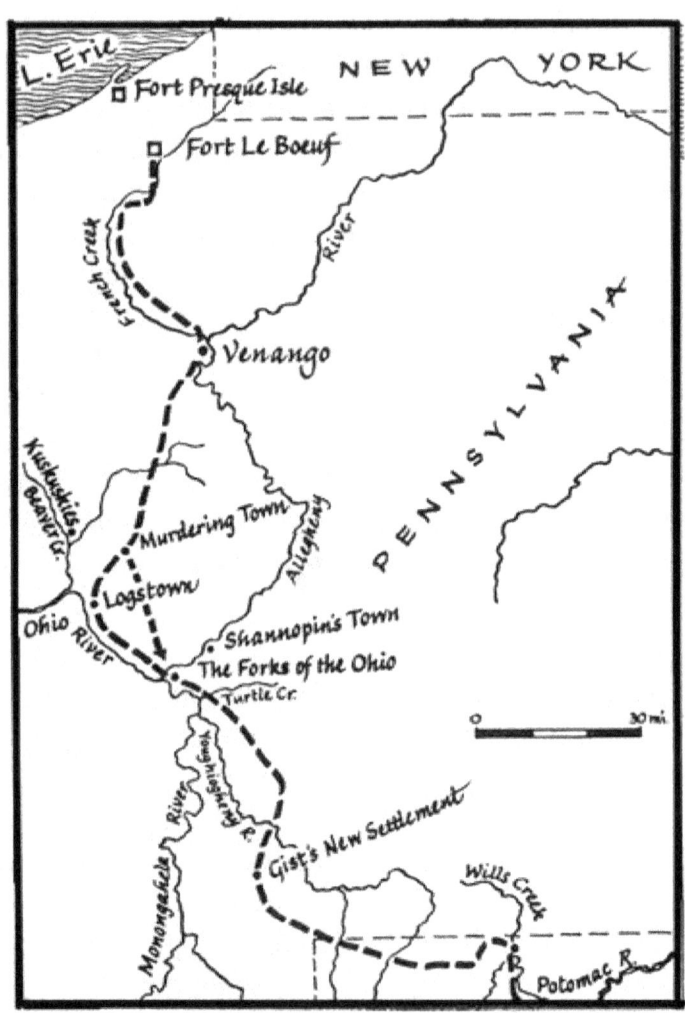

The Gist and Washington Journey 1753-54

SIX

Soon after returning east, Christopher Gist was named as an Ohio Company agent to the forthcoming Logstown Conference. Gist had no official status other than being the representative of one of the vested interests (the Ohio Company); his duties were somewhat like those of a present-day lobbyist. The meeting was planned to begin in late April but did not get under way until the first of June because Tanaghrisson, Half-King of the Senecas, was late in arriving. The Indians in attendance were representatives of the Six Nations, the Delaware, Shawnees, and Wyandot. Because the conference was held under the sponsorship of the Colony of Virginia, Pennsylvania sent only George Croghan as an "unofficial" delegate.

After the opening ceremonies were concluded, presents were distributed to the tribes in attendance. The first few days of the Conference were occupied with a common exchange of good wishes, as well as preparing the Indians for the more serious issues. Besides questions of land, stress was placed upon the assertion the French wanted to exterminate the Indians while the English wanted to live in union with them. (To be fair to the French, the truth is the situation was quite the opposite.)

On June 11, the real talks began with Tanaghrisson refusing to accept the notion that land west of the Alleghenies had been granted to Virginia under the Treaty of Lancaster. However, because Indians feared the French, it was agreeable for the Ohio Company to build a fort at the Forks of the Ohio River (Pittsburgh) to keep supplies, guns, ammunition, food, and merchandise there. When Gist asked if he was granting permission to build a fort for defense and a settlement, Tanaghrisson said, "Only for defense." At this point, Gist went to work as a negotiator and by late afternoon talked Tanaghrisson into allowing an English settlement east of the Forks of the Ohio. Thus, the new agreement recognized Virginia's claims under the Treaty of Lancaster and guaranteed the Ohio Company the right to establish settlements which would be unmolested by Indians.

As part of the Logstown Agreement, the Indians insisted that agents not be allowed to sell liquor to the Indians because of the disastrous effects "fire water" had upon their warriors. Also, the Indians asked Virginia and the Ohio Company to appoint only three agents to conduct trade and business with them, with one being Christopher Gist.

*   *   *

From 1752 to 1755 Gist engaged in a variety of activities: surveyor, road builder, recruitment office, and guide. However, the Logstown Treaty granted the Ohio Company permission to establish a settlement and Gist was the man assigned the task. Gist chose a piece of land located in the Monongahela Valley in a region east of the Forks of the Ohio. In present day terms it was located in Dunbar Township, PA, about six miles from Uniontown. Gist's home became a famous frontier post and was referred to as "Gist's Settlement" or "Gist's Plantation," while Gist himself called it "Monongahela." By 1754, Gist was heading a thriving community of at least eleven other families. As would be expected, the settlement included a storehouse for Ohio Company goods. Today, there is a Gist's Plantation historical marker located on US 119, 4.5 miles SW of Connellsville, Pennsylvania. The marker text reads:

Photographed By Mike Wintermantel

"**The general location of Gist's plantation** is known to be in the vicinity of Mount Braddock, Pennsylvania. A marker along Route 119 at Latitude 39.954968°, Longitude -79.651651° commemorates the settlement. Many sources indicate that Gist's cabin was located at the site of Isaac Meason's mansion, which is located at Latitude 39.953913°, Longitude -79.648248°" (Lannie Dietle).

Mr. Dietle became interested in this subject as a result of Arthur P. Freed's article in the February 1966 issue of the "Laurel Messenger". Freed disputes the Meason house theory, because of the lack of a spring. Braddock road historian Robert Bantz concurs, writing the following to Mr. Dietle on March 17, 2013: "Many folks, including many from Fort Necessity, believe his cabin was on the present Isaac Meason mansion property that was built on Gist's land... I searched the entire area. I could never find a source of water on that site. It just always made sense to me that he would settle along the stream..."

After viewing Mr. Dietle's YouTube presentation, and reading his paper on the subject, I am convinced his conclusions are right as to the true location as to Gist's plantation.

Identifying the site of Christopher Gist's cabin

www.youtube.com/watch?v=Vzmndr4kkbU

The white paper Mr. Dietle refers to can be found at

https://korns.org/misc/Gist_cabin_location.pdf

The Historical Marker Database, Gist's Plantation

www.hmdb.org/m.asp?m=59677

In August 1753, when Gist learned the French were building a fort at Presque Isle (Erie, Pennsylvania), and a road from the fort south to French Creek, he decided to proceed to Williamsburg and relate the news to Governor Dinwiddie. After learning of the French encroachment, on October 31, 1753, he commissioned young George Washington as an envoy to deliver a message of protest to the French commander at Fort Le Boeuf. Gist at the same time was selected to act as Washington's guide. This journey as Washington's guide may be called Gist's most significant undertaking. All together there would be eight men in their party.

On November 17, they arrived at Gist's Plantation, where they remained until November 19. On the twenty-second, the travelers reached John Fraser's cabin, where they borrowed a canoe. (John Fraser, a Pennsylvania gunsmith and Indian trader, had established a trading post at Venango in the 1740s. Forced to leave by a French force that occupied the post in 1753, he resumed his trading operations at another trading post he had already established at the mouth of Turtle Creek on the Monongahela about ten miles above the present site of Pittsburgh.) Gist and Washington sent their baggage down the Monongahela River in charge of two or three members of the party, and they set out on horseback. On the next day, Washington viewed for the first time the forks of the Monongahela and Allegheny Rivers.

They continued their journey to Logstown to meet with Tanaghrisson, who was also known as the Half-King, before moving on to Ft. LeBoeuf. (Those Iroquois who had migrated to the Ohio Country were generally known as "Mingos", and Tanaghrisson emerged as a Mingo leader. However, when an important decision needed to be made, the leading women would discuss the matter. The men would then take the women's opinions into consideration. This is the reason he was known as the Half-King).

It was the Half-King that most colonial visitors to the Ohio Country sought information, advice, and assistance. When Washington was sent to Fort LeBoeuf, few whites had ventured north of Logstown, so Gist and Washington needed a guide. They knew the Half-King not only knew the landscape, but because he was as a Mingo leader, he could assure them safe passage.

Washington described their meeting:

About 3 o'Clock this Evening the Half-King came to Town; I went up & invited him & Davison privately to my Tent, & desir'd him to relate some of the Particulars of his Journey to the French Commandant, & reception there, & to give me an Account of the Way & Distance. He told me that the nearest & levelest Way was now impassable, by reason of the many large miry Savannas; that we must be oblig'd to go by Venango, & shou'd not get to the near Fort under 5 or 6 Nights Sleep, good Traveling.

Once Fraser was forced to move, Venango became an important French trading and supply post at the juncture of French Creek and the Allegheny River. It is now Franklin, PA.

Gist's description of the journey from Logstown to Venango reads:

Friday 30—We set out, and the Half-King and two old men and one young warrior, with us. At night we encamped at the Murthering town, about fifteen miles, on a branch of Great Beaver Creek. Got some corn and dried meat.

Saturday 1—December—Set out, and at night encamped at the crossing of Beaver creek from the Kaskuskies to Venango about thirty miles. The next day rain; our Indians went out a hunting; they killed two bucks. Had rain all day.

Monday 3—We set out and travelled all day. Encamped at night on one of the head branches of Great Beaver creek about twenty-two miles.

Tuesday [4]—Set out about fifteen miles, to the town of Venango, where we were kindly and complaisantly received by Monsieur Joncaire, the French interpreter for the Six Nations

According to Gist's diary, the party left Venango on December 6th. His entries for the journey to Fort Le Boeuf read as follows:

Thursday 6—We set out late in the day accompanied by the French General and four servants or soldiers, and

Friday 7—All encamped at Sugar creek, five miles from Venango. The creek being very high we were obliged to carry all our baggage over on trees, and swim our horses. The Major and I went first over, with our boots on.

Saturday [8]—We set out and travelled twenty-five miles to Cussewago, an old Indian town.

Sunday 9—We set out, left one of our horses here that could travel no further. This day we travelled to the big crossing, about fifteen miles, and encamped, our Indians went out to look out logs to make a raft; but as the water was high, and there were other creeks to cross, we concludeed to keep up this side the creek.

Monday 10—Set out, travelled about eight miles, and encamped. Our Indians killed a bear. Here we had a creek to cross, very deep; we got over on a tree, and got our goods over.

Tuesday 11—We set out, travelled about fifteen miles to the French fort, the sun being set. Our interpreter gave the commandant notice of our being over the creek; upon which he sent several officers to conduct us to the fort, and they received us with a great deal of complaisance [marked by an inclination to please or oblige].

"*Wednesday 12—The Major gave the passport, showed his commission, and offered the Governor's letter to the commandant; but he desired not to receive them, until the other commander from Lake Erie came, whom he had sent for, and expected next day by twelve o'clock.*

Thursday 13—The other General came. The Major delivered the letter, and desired a speedy answer; the time of year and business required it.

Portions of the *Letter from Virginia's Governor Dinwiddie to the French Commander in the Ohio Country, October, 1753.*

* * *

Sir,

The lands upon the River Ohio, in the western parts of the Colony of Virginia, are so notoriously known to be the property of the Crown of Great Britain that it is a matter of equal concern and surprise to me, to hear that a body of French forces are erecting fortresses and making settlements upon that river, within his Majesty's dominions.

The many and repeated complaints I have received of these acts of hostility lay me under the necessity of sending, in the name of the King, my master, the bearer hereof, George Washington, Esq.

However, sir, in obedience to my instructions, it becomes my duty to require your peaceable departure; and that you would forbear prosecuting a purpose so interruptive of the harmony and good understanding, which his Majesty is desirous to continue and cultivate with the most Christian King.

I have the honor to be,

Your very humble,

ROBERT DINWIDDIE.

* * *

Le Gardeur de Saint-Pierre forwarded Dinwiddie's letter to Governor Duquesne on December 22nd. The governor found the claims of the Virginians to be without foundation; the area incontestably belonged to the French.

Here Gist described the return trip from Fort Le Boeuf to Venango:

Friday 14—We set out with two canoes, one for our Indians, and the other for ourselves. Our horses we had sent away some days before, to wait at Venango.

Sunday 16—We set out by water about sixteen miles, and encamped.

Monday 17—We set out, came to our Indians' camp. They were out hunting; they killed three bears...

Tuesday 18— [F]inding the waters lower very fast, were obliged to go and leave our Indians.

Wednesday 19 - Thursday 20—We set out about seven or eight miles, and encamped. The next day [we traveled] About twenty miles, where we were stopped by ice, and worked until night.

Friday 21—The ice was so hard we could not break our way through, but were obliged to haul our vessels across a point of land and put them in the creek again. This night we encamped about twenty miles above Venango.

Saturday 22—Set out. The creek began to be very low and we were forced to get out, to keep our canoe from over-setting, several times; the water freezing to our clothes;

(This was the first time in his journals that Gist allowed himself a bit of humor.)

and we had the pleasure of seeing the French overset, and the brandy and wine floating in the creek, and run by them, and left them to shift for themselves. Came to Venango, and met with our people and horses.

On their return trip, using his woodsman's instinct and experience, Gist saved the young major's life twice.

To the dismay of the group, their horses, which had earlier been sent down from Fort Le Bœuf, had not sufficiently recovered their strength. [Could not dig through the snow for grass or water] The group started out on the horses anyway but soon realized that their mounts and pack horses were in such bad shape that their progress was drastically slowed. Washington and Gist dismounted and spread the baggage among all the horses in order to lighten the loads on each, but it didn't help much. The men soon found it impossible to remain mounted and were forced to travel on foot while leading their exhausted animals.

Washington grew frustrated by the slow pace of travel and here is where inexperience and youthful recklessness caught up with him. To make up for lost time, he decided to split up his party, leaving most of the gear behind with his men, while he and Gist continued alone through the woods with no guide and no protection except their own muskets. [Tanaghrisson did not join them on this part of the trip.] Gist:

Monday, [December] 24, [1753]—Here Major Washington set out on foot in Indian dress. Our horses grew weak, that we were mostly obliged to travel on foot, and had snow all day.

Wednesday 26.—The Major desired me to set out on foot, and leave our company, as the creeks were frozen, and our horses could make but little way. Indeed, I was unwilling he should undertake such a travel, who had never been used to walking before this time. But as he insisted on it, I set out with our packs, like Indians, and travelled eighteen miles. That night we lodged at an Indian cabin, and the Major was much fatigued. It was very cold; all the small runs were frozen, that we could hardly get water to drink.

Gist had doubts about young Washington's ability to traverse the rugged wilderness on foot in the depths of winter. Indeed, it would be challenging for an experienced frontiersman, but for the inexperienced twenty-one-year-old Washington it would be a grueling winter trek fraught with perils. The young major, though strong, was more used to covering distances on horseback than on foot.

Thursday 27—We rose early in the morning, and set out about two o'clock. Got to the Murthering town, on the southeast fork of Beaver creek. Here we met with an Indian, whom I thought I had seen at Joncaire's, at Venango, when on our journey up to the French fort. This fellow called me by my Indian name [Annosanah], and pretended to be glad to see me. He asked us several questions, as how we came to travel on foot, when we left Venango, where we parted with our horses ... Major Washington insisted on travelling on the nearest way to forks of Alleghany. We asked the Indian if he could go with us, and show us the nearest way. The Indian seemed very glad and ready to go with us. Upon which we set out, and the Indian took the Major's pack. We travelled very brisk for eight or ten miles.]T]he Major's feet grew very sore, and he very weary, and the Indian steered too much north-eastwardly.

The Major desired to encamp, to which the Indian ... pressed us to keep on, telling us that there were Ottawa Indians in these woods, and they would scalp us so we should go to his cabin, where we should be safe.

I thought very ill of the fellow, but did not care to let the Major know I mistrusted him. But he soon mistrusted him as much as I ... [for he] steered us more northwardly. We grew uneasy ... then the Major said he would stop at the next water, and we desired the Indian to stop at the next water. But before we came to water, we came to a clear meadow; it was very light, and snow on the ground. The Indian made a stop, turned about; the Major saw him point his gun toward us and fire. Said the Major, 'Are you shot?' 'No,' said I. Upon which the Indian ran forward to a big standing white oak, and to loading his gun; but we were soon with him. I would have killed him; but the Major would not suffer me to kill him ... The Major or I always stood by the guns; we made him make a fire for us by a little run, as if we intended to sleep there. I said to the Major, 'As you will not have him killed, we must get him away, and then we must travel all night.'

Washington feared killing the man would spark hostilities between the British and Indians, so he let him go. He immediately regretted the decision—realizing in all likelihood, the whole tribe would descend upon them.

[W]hen we made a fire, set our compass, and fixed our course, and travelled all night, and in the morning we were on the head of Piney creek.

Friday 28 — We travelled all the next day... [In all about 36 hours]

Two days later on Saturday, December 29, 1753, Washington and Gist reached the west bank of the Allegheny River about two miles above Shannopin's Town and approximately five miles from the Forks. They had hoped to be able to walk across the frozen river to the east bank, but the solid ice only extended about fifty yards from either shore with a swift current and treacherous ice floes in the middle of the river. They decided to build a raft to get to the other side.

Washington's account captured the perilous endeavor in more detail:

There was no Way for getting over but on a Raft: Which we set about, with but one poor Hatchet, and finished just after Sun-setting. This was a whole Day's Work: we next got it launched, and went on Board of it: Then set off. But before we were Half Way over, we were jammed in the Ice, in such a Manner that we expected our Raft to sink, and ourselves to perish. I put out my setting Pole to try to stop the Raft, that the Ice might pass by; when the Rapidity of the Stream threw it with so much Violence against the Pole, that it jirked me out into ten Feet Water: But I fortunately saved myself by catching hold of one of the Raft Logs. Notwithstanding all our Efforts we could not get the Raft to either Shore; but were obliged, as we were near an island, to quit our Raft and make to it.

Coming ashore on the little island in the Allegheny River, the two soaked and freezing men were saved only by Gist's frontier savvy and his ability to quickly start a fire and construct a crude shelter. The night was bitterly cold, and Gist, who primarily tended the fire and worked to dry their garments, bore the brunt of the elements. Washington wrote that. *The Cold was so extremely severe, that Mr. Gist had all his fingers, and some of his Toes frozen.*

On Sunday, December 30, 1753, after leaving the little island, Washington and Gist traveled ten miles to John Fraser's cabin at the mouth of Turtle Creek.

On New Year's Day, 1754, they set out for Gist's plantation where they arrived the second of January. Here Washington purchased a horse and saddle from one of the settlers and continued to Williamsburg. On January 16, Washington presented Governor Dinwiddie the unfavorable reply of the French commander:

As I have the honor of commanding here in chief, Mr. Washington delivered me the letter which you wrote to the commander of the French troops ... As to the Summons you send me to retire, I do not think myself obliged to obey it; whatever may be your Instructions, I am here by Virtue of the Orders of my General ; and I intreat you, Sir, not to doubt one Moment, but that I am determin'd to conform myself to them with all the Exactness and Resolution which can be expected from the best Officer ... I have made it a particular duty to receive Mr. Washington with the distinction owing to your dignity, his position, and his own great merit. I trust that he will do me justice in that regard with you, and that he will make known to you the profound respect with which I am, Sir, Your most humble and most obedient servant,

Your most humble, and most obedient Servant,

                    Legardeur de Saint-Pierre,

It was during this trip that Washington and Gist formed a friendship that lasted until Gist's death. More importantly, it is unimaginable what kind of nation would have emerged had Washington been killed.

SEVEN

Even before he learned of the French refusal to abandon the Ohio Valley, in January 1754, Governor Dinwiddie sent a small force of Virginia soldiers to build a fort at the Forks of the Ohio. The stockade was barely started when the French forced the Virginians to retreat and proceeded to build their own larger fort on the site. The French called it Fort Duquesne in honor of the Marquis de Duquesne, the new governor of New France.

In early April, George Washington, newly commissioned lieutenant colonel in the Virginia Regiment, started westward from Alexandria to build a road to Redstone Creek, present day Brownsville, PA, on the Monongahela. He was then to help defend the English fort on the Ohio. When Washington reached Wills Creek, he learned the fort was in French hands. Despite hearing this, he resolved to push on to Redstone Creek. By late May of 1754, Washington had reached a large natural clearing known as the Great Meadows. He made this his base camp. Grass there could provide food for his animals, and water was readily available.

As soon as the French completed building "Fort Duquesne," it became their seat of organized action. One of the first acts of the French commander Contrecoeur was to send Lieutenant La Force with a number of men to scout the country to the south for intelligence concerning English settlers. Under the pretense of hunting for deserters, he came to Gist's place, now a trading post, in the early part of May, but continued scouting the surrounding country. At noon on May 26, La Force's party returned and asked Gist the whereabouts of Seneca Chief Half King, Tanaghrisson. Gist pleaded ignorance and with that La Force departed. Gist trailed them to within five miles of the Great Meadows, where Washington was encamped. Very early the next morning he arrived at the Great Meadows, where he related to Washington what had taken place. This alarmed Washington so he wrote a letter to Governor Dinwiddie, which he gave to Gist to deliver.

In Gist's absence, Washington received word from Tanacharison, that a party of French soldiers were camped in a ravine not far from his position. On the stormy night of May 27th, 1754, Washington and about 40 men began an all-night march to confront the French and learn their intentions. About dawn, Washington met again with Tanacharison and discussed how to establish a parlay with the French.

Because the French commander neglected to post sentries, Washington and his men easily surrounded the unsuspecting French. A shot was fired, no one really knows by whom, and soon the peaceful glen was filled with the crash of musketry and the smell of powder. The skirmish lasted about 15 minutes. When it was over, 13 Frenchmen were dead and 21 captured. One escaped and made his way back to Fort Duquesne. One of the individuals killed was Ensign Joseph Coulon de Villiers de Jumonville, who was on the same type of diplomatic assignment Washington had been on earlier. Washington's casualties were one man killed and two or three wounded.

In the aftermath of the skirmish, Gist's plantation became a supply center for Washington's troops. However, fearing a large French force was about to descend upon them, it was decided to fall back to the Great Meadows. There Washington ordered the construction of a makeshift stockade named Fort Necessity. When over nine hundred French and Indians attacked, Washington was outnumbered and agreed to surrender the fort and troops on the condition that he and his men retire with the honors of war. What Washington did not realize, because he could not read French, was that the surrender document stated that he, personally, had assassinated de Jumonville. Gist, by this time had returned from Alexandria, and took part in the battle. The French, because of Gist's involvement, upon their victorious retreat, burned Gist's plantation and the Ohio Company's store-house. From there the French continued on to Redstone Creek, where they destroyed the Ohio Company's store-house there. For all practical purposes, this was to become the death knell of the Ohio Company of Virginia.

*   *   *

Angered over his losses to the French, Gist was willing to join any British expedition that might set out for the Ohio Country. When the Crown appointed General Edward Braddock to lead a campaign against Fort Duquesne, Gist became Braddock's guide and leader of scouts. Sadly though, Braddock ignored warnings from Gist, other scouts, and Washington, and walked right into a French and French-Indians ambush. The British army was crushed, and Braddock was mortally wounded. With Braddock incapacitated, Washington took control by riding back and forth across the battlefield, rallying troops, and bringing a sense of order to the melee. Upon Braddock's death, command passed to Colonel Thomas Dunbar, whose troops were held in reserve during the massacre. Washington, Gist, and others expected Dunbar to reorganize the army for a second attempt at taking Fort Duquesne. However, Dunbar's troops became so panic-stricken when they heard stories of Indian scalping, the colonel found it necessary to march them directly to winter quarters in Philadelphia— turning a blind eye to Virginians' request for assistance in guarding their frontier.

So impressed with how Washington (and Gist) salvaged Braddock's disastrous campaign, Governor Dinwiddie gave him command of the Virginia Regiment in 1755. The Regiment was made up of a body of standing troops who formed a more disciplined and dependable body than the colonial militia or rangers. The number of companies varied based on need but there were two companies which deserve mention. One was the Troop of Horses Company. Their duty was to clear the woods of hostile Indians or French. The other Company was the Company of Scouts—which during Washington's tenure, was under the command of Christopher Gist. As you will read, their function and duties were unique.

Two orders from George Washington to Christopher Gist:

October 10, 1755

Before I got to Williamsburgh, ... I succeeded in procuring the only Commission that was vacant, i.e. to be Captain of a Company of Scouts ... It is intended, that your Company shall consist as much of active woodsmen, capable of something adequate to your names; I must therefore desire you will Repair immediately thither, in order to receive Money and Instructions to Recruit them...

I doubt not but you have heard of the Ravages committed by our inhuman Foes, on the back inhabitants; I am now upon my March against them, with full hopes, that I shall be able to get Satisfaction for their cruel Barbarities. Never were Indians more wanted than at this time; I have therefore sent to Montour, inviting him, and all he can bring, and should be glad that you would come that way, and use all your interest ... to engage his coming; I will promise if he brings many, to do something handsome for him...

October 18, 1755.

1. You are hereby ordered to Repair to Harris's Ferry, and other places where the Indondians are upon the

Susquehanna, and to use your utmost endeavours to engage them to come and lodge their Wives and Families in our Forts, and assist us in fighting their own Battles.

2ly. You are, so soon as you arrive at the first of those Town or Parties, to hire an Indian to go Express to Captain Andrew Montour; to whom you are to write, desiring him to come and assist you, in bringing them to Fort Cumberland.

3ly. You may assure the Indians that they shall meet with plenty of Provisions, &c. and that we shall take every opportunity to testify the Love we bear them.

4ly. If they should want Horses &c. to assist them along, you are to Hire; this, with all other reasonable charges, will be allowed you.

5ly. You may acquaint the Belt of Wampum, and other Chiefs, that I have complied with their Requests in letting the Governor of Virginia know, that the Shawnees and Delawares have taken the Hatchet against us; and of the French Scheme in setting the Southern Indians against us; which will now be prevented.

6ly. You may also promise Captain Montour from me, that if he will get and bring a Company of Indians consisting of Sixty men (which is the number of our Companies) that he shall have a Captains Commission, and receive ten shillings a day, and be paid once a month regularly; and if he brings more Men, he will meet with further encouragement.

7ly. If you should meet with any likely young Fellows (Woods-men) you are to enlist them for His Majestys' Service, in your own Company: observing always the Instructions given you for that purpose. Given &c.

Harris' Ferry Marker
Erected by
The Pennsylvania Historical Commission
September 24, 1915.

On the bank of the Susquehanna River, was the landing place of Harris' Ferry, the most historic crossing place on the Susquehanna. A great part of the early migration into Western Pennsylvania and the Ohio Valley passed this way. The Ferry-right was first granted to John Harris, father of the founder of Harrisburg, in December, 1733. For over half a century the site of Harrisburg was known as Harris' Ferry.

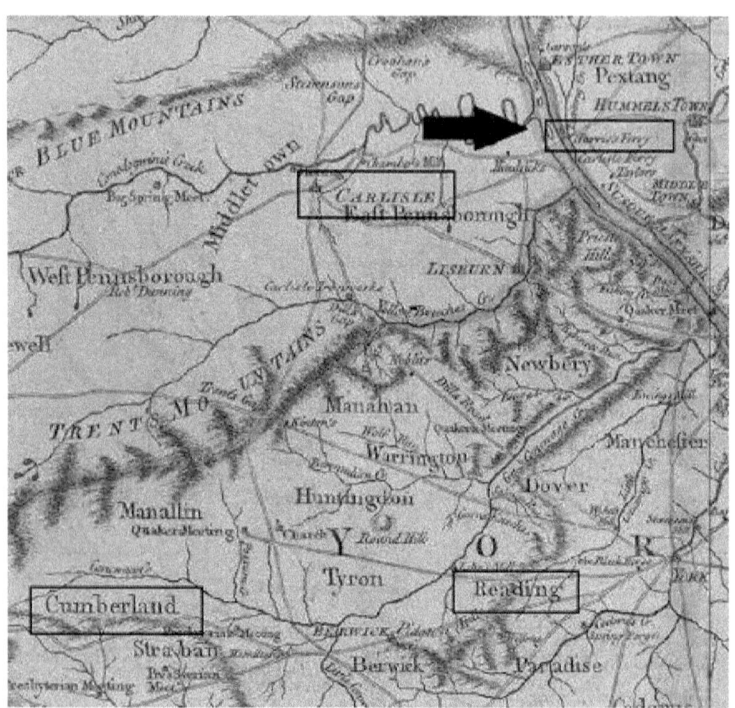

EIGHT

Violent native resistance to Euro-American occupation of the Ohio Valley characterized the settlement period from the 1750s to the 1790s. When European or colonial governments were directly engaged, specific conflicts acquired a formal name, such as the French and Indian War (1754–63); raids and counterraids by small groups of fighters were typical of the period. Generally, the conflict exhibited the classic forms of guerrilla war: raids, ambushes, sneak attacks, massacres, and atrocities on both sides. Indian raids usually struck at the western edge of white settlement, which meant that the fighting shifted from east to west: and no part of the frontier was entirely safe until Indians began withdrawing from their Ohio homelands after the Treaty of Greenville in 1795.

Euro-American authorities frequently engaged native leaders in negotiations, seeking to head off problems short of warfare. Another defensive strategy was the building of frontier forts, which were of two types: garrisons established at key points near the western edge of settlement, such as Fort Pitt and neighborhood forts in which settlers could seek shelter in times of Indian alarm. "Forting" became a formative frontier experience for generations of settlers.

When whites went on the offensive, it was usually in direct immediate response to an Indian raid that had resulted in captives, or it was a larger military expedition that sought to find and destroy the Indian villages in Ohio from which the native raiders came. As often as not, these largescale expeditions were unsuccessful, as in Braddock's Campaign.

*   *   *

From 1755 to 1757, repeated raids by Indians caused much hardship on the frontier, and it frequently went unpunished. An expedition sent against the destroyers of settlements along the Roanoke River was soundly defeated. Then, just eighteen miles from Winchester, a detachment was defeated with a loss of nearly thirty soldiers. Records suggest Gist engaged in several of these skirmishes, but his main occupations remained recruiting and serving as a messenger for Washington.

The type of violence and bloodshed between Indians and settlers was due to neither the colonies nor the mother country developing anything that remotely resembled a satisfactory Indian policy. In the south, Virginia and the Carolinas, with their sea-to-sea charters, endured all sorts of quarrels between whites and Indians. Also, conflicting views held by Governor Dinwiddie of Virginia and Governor James Glen of South Carolina, led to disputes between the southern colonies.

Both men saw eye to eye on the necessity of expelling the French from the Ohio Valley; however, they disagreed as to the means of obtaining this end. In contrast to his contemporaries who thought the best defense was to set the Indian tribes against one another, Governor Glen saw the French as the true enemy and sought to unite all the tribes friendly to the English. Dinwiddie felt all Indians should be manipulated to the advantage of the British Empire. To mediate between the two men, and present a single spokesperson to Native Americans, Gist was appointed Deputy Agent of Indian Affairs for the Southern Department in July 1757.

Gist was perfectly qualified for the position. To show his confidence in Gist, George Washington wrote:

I know of no person so well qualified ... He has had extensive dealings with the Indians, is in great esteem among them; well acquainted with their manners and customs—is indefatigable and patient ... Most excellent qualities indeed, where Indians are concerned! And, for his capacity, honesty and Zeal, I dare venture to engage.

G:W.
May 30th 1757.

Since moving from Baltimore to the Yankin River in North Carolina, he had been in almost daily contact with the Indians. His expedition to the Ohio, the Logstown Conference, scouting activities, and many similar duties made him one of the colony's foremost authorities of Native Americans. From 1750-1755 Gist showed remarkable skill in keeping the Ohio Indians from aligning with the French. Finally, during the months he had been captain of the Scouts, he had been Washington's chief assistant in Indian relations.

In assuming his new post on January 1, 1758, Gist took up residence in Winchester, Virginia. From there he had several responsibilities:

1. Pay the Indians for debts incurred by Washington and other officers in the Virginian regiments;

2. Take stock of Indian presents (guns, gunpowder, bullets, clasp and scalping knives, blankets, tomahawks, calico

cloth, shirts, coats, needles, brass kettles, silver brooches, red war paint, wampum, silver, etc.) on hand, determine what presents would be needed to assure a large supply of Indians for the upcoming Forbes campaigns on hand;

3. Submit quarterly reports of presents awarded to Indians--this would make it possible to have a steady supply of presents to keep Indians happy;

4. Establish two forts on the Virginia frontier: one at Winchester where he was stationed, and the other at the head of the Roanoke River. The Indians' scouting parties were to assemble at these forts and be fitted out for war;

5. Assist the British troops when they should start actions against the French (i.e. the Forbes Campaign) by supplying them with Indian fighters and scouts, and report anything of importance with respect to the enemy;

6. Have all commanders at Virginia's two forts direct the Catawba and Cherokee Indians from the Carolinas to go along the western fringe of settlements by way of the heads of the Roanoke and James Rivers. This route would prevent their passing through Virginia on their way to the northwest frontier (instead of passing through the heart of Virginia's settled region where they had the habit of molesting settlements by stealing food, supplies, and horses, and spreading infectious disease).

Gist's actual work as an Indian agent, while dangerous and difficult, was quite matter of fact and routine. The frustrating feature of his work was the never-ending contest between himself and the government of Virginia. This became an on-going struggle to secure adequate money and gifts for the Indians while Virginia was careful not to spend any more unnecessary money. Virginia's leaders seemed to believe it might be possible to exploit the Indians by being slow, even careless, in fulfilling promises made. The patronizing officials naively believed they could rely upon a lack of intelligence on the part of the "savages" to keep them from divining the true situation. The situation grew so bad that even George Washington weighed in on the issue to Governor Dinwiddie:

I applied to Captain Gist in their behalf, and told him I must represent the matter to your Honor. But he assures me that he has neither goods to reward them, money to procure them, or even an interpreter, which totally incapacitates him for doing any kind of service. If so (which I have no reason to doubt) it is surprising, that any man shou'd be entrusted with the negotiating of such important affairs, and not be possessed of the means to accomplish the undertaking. By which he, and several others, who received high pay from Virginia, are not only rendered useless, but our interests with those Indians is at the brink of destruction. Whenever a party of them arrive here, they immediately apply to me; but I have neither anything to give them, nor any right to do it.

As noted by historian Kenneth P. Bailey, Gist was given a job fifty [men] could not handle. Although neither the Virginia Council nor the British military leaders had good words to say of Gist's work, people who knew the frontier situation felt differently. George Mercer, treasurer of the Ohio Company, seemed to have believed Gist accomplished much; he even liked the way Gist kept his accounts. As shown, Washington was sympathetic, and while finding no reason to express praise, he undoubtedly felt it was not necessary and remained loyal to the end.

Smallpox was rampant among the Indians in 1759. One newspaper account claimed that nearly one-half of the entire Catawba tribe succumbed to the disease. While escorting a party of Catawba Indians between Williamsburg and Winchester, Christopher Gist contracted the disease and died on July 25, 1759.

*   *   *

It is impossible to read any historical account of settling the region from the Blue Ridge Mountains to the Falls of the Ohio without coming across Christopher Gist's name. This, then, raises the question as to why he has been so under-appreciated by historians. Here are some thoughts I have on the subject:

Regardless of how we want to think of Gist as a great American explorer, the truth is, first, he was British, and second, his explorations of the Ohio Country were not for the colonies of Virginia or Maryland, but as part of a corporation enterprise.

When Gist died, his surviving children did not realize their father's importance; consequently, they saw no reason to write about him.

The journals Gist wrote for the Ohio Company remained out of the American publics' hands until 1893—nearly 150 years after they were written—until printed, in full, by William M. Darlington.

And even if Gist had achieved relative fame during his lifetime, it was soon overshadowed by the American Revolution, the Founding Fathers, and the Lewis and Clark expedition.

Gist Biography from Appleton's Cyclopedia of American Biography Vol. 2, 1887

GIST, Christopher, scout. He was summoned from his home on the Yadkin in North Carolina by the Ohio company, an association of English merchants and Virginia planters, to whom had been given a royal grant to examine the western country "as far as the falls of the Ohio," to mark the passes in the mountains, trace the course of rivers, and observe the strength and numbers of the Indian nations. On 31 Oct., 1750, he left the shores of the Potomac. He crossed the Alleghanies and journeyed in February, 1751, to the Miami river, holding conferences with the various Indian tribes, but principally with the chief of the Miamis. During the latter meeting four ambassadors from the French were announced, but, after a deliberation, an alliance was formed with Gist, as the representative of the English. On 1 March, Gist continued his tour, descending the Miami to the Ohio; thence ascending the valley of the Kentucky, he found a pass to the Bluestone, and returned by way of the Roanoke. In 1753 the Ohio company opened a road into the western valley, and Gist established a plantation near the Youghiogheny. In November of that year hostilities were threatened between the French and English; and George Washington, then just twenty-one, but thoroughly familiar with the wilderness, was selected as an envoy from Gov. Dinwiddie, of Virginia, to make a winter journey to the streams of Lake Erie. With Christopher Gist as his guide he set out. In nine days they had reached the junction of the Alleghany and Monongahela rivers, and on 23 Nov., 1753, swam their horses across the Alleghany, and wrapped themselves in their blankets for the night. Their journey ended at Waterford, near the shores of Lake Erie, where they were not courteously received. They hastened their return, and the day after Christmas were fired upon by an Indian in ambush. " I would have killed him," wrote Gist, " but Washington forbade." They took him prisoner instead. Dismissing their captive at dusk, they travelled all night and next day, resting at dark under a huge tree. The despatches were delivered, and a fort was established at the junction of the rivers which Washington and Gist had crossed, where Pittsburg now stands. It was afterward, 17 April, seized by the French, and named Fort Duquesne. Washington hastened

forward, Gist acting as his scout, and on 27 April the latter announced that the French were within five miles of the American camp. An engagement followed, and the French were beaten. Gist's subsequent history is unknown.

Appendix I

Extracts from the History of Cincinnati and the Territory of Ohio

Adolphus Eberhardt Jones, 1888. Retrieved from https://archive.org.

CHAPTER II.

Organization of the Old Ohio Company — Lawrence and Augustine Washington, Brothers of General George Washington, Members of the Company — Lawrence Washington's Liberal Policy.

EARLY in 1749, a grand scheme to colonize the western country was conceived by some of the most prominent men of Virginia, among whom were Thomas Lee, President of the Council of Virginia; Augustine and Lawrence Washington, elder brothers of George Washington; and John Hanbury, a wealthy merchant of London.

An association was organized by these gentlemen under the name of the Ohio Company, now known as the Old Ohio Company, in contradistinction to another which adopted the same title, organized in Boston in 1786, composed principally of ex-revolutionary soldiers.

The mother country encouraged this enterprise as one which would, if successful, enable it to possess itself of the coveted prize, and thereby more firmly establish the claims of England, by actual occupancy.

A charter was issued to the company, and a grant made of six hundred thousand acres of land on the southeast side of the Ohio River, between the Monongahela and Kanawha Rivers, with the privilege, however, of taking a part of it on the northwest side of the Ohio. The conditions upon which the charter was issued, were that the company should settle one hundred families on the grant within seven years from the date of the charter, build a fort and maintain a sufficient force to protect the settlers, who were to pay no quit rent for ten years.

Thomas Lee, one of the Commissioners who had made the treaty with the Iroquois at Lancaster in 1744, was the leader in the movement until his death, which occurred soon after the organization of the company. After his death the management of its affairs devolved upon Lawrence Washington, the elder of the brothers.

The wise and liberal policy adopted by Mr. Washington as manager gave great promise of success to the enterprise, and preparations were actively inaugurated to perfect the necessary arrangements to take possession and commence the settlements. It was his desire to form colonies of Germans from Pennsylvania; but here a difficulty presented itself which could not be easily overcome. The grant was within the jurisdiction of Virginia, in which the Church of England was established by law and maintained by tithes, and therefore settlers would be compelled to pay parish rates for the maintenance of the clergy; and the Germans of Pennsylvania, being dissenters, were not willing to submit to this condition. Lawrence Washington sought to have them relieved from this tax, but without success. A single quotation from his writings at the time will serve to show his liberal and enlightened views:

"It has ever been my opinion," said he, " and hope it ever will be, that restraints on conscience are cruel in regard to those on whom they are imposed, and injurious to the country imposing them. England, Holland and Prussia, I may quote as examples, and much more Pennsylvania, which has flourished under delightful liberty so as to become the admiration of every man who considers the short time it has been settled.

"This colony — Virginia — was greatly settled in the latter part of Charles the First's time, and during the usurpation, by the zealous churchmen, and that spirit which was then brought in, has ever since continued, so that, except a few Quakers, we have no dissenters. But what has been the consequence? We have increased by slow degrees, while our neighboring colonies, whose natural advantages are greatly inferior to ours, have become populous."

While it is true that Lord Baltimore had promulgated and established the principles of religious freedom in Maryland, and it was tolerated in Pennsylvania previous to this, still the sentiments expressed in the foregoing quotations from Mr. Washington are remarkable as coming from a member of the Established Church of England ; and it is a striking coincidence that they should be almost identical with the principles contained in the ordinance of 1787, under which the Northwest Territory was organized nearly thirty years afterward, and in the Constitution of the United States and State of Ohio, leaving to every man the right to worship God according to the dictates of his own conscience.

General George Washington was then a youth under the guidance and influence, in a great measure, of his brother, Lawrence, who took a parental interest in the education and direction of his youth. May not the early teachings he then received have resulted in that liberal policy and love of liberty he ever manifested in his public life, and developed that remarkable character which so eminently qualified him to lead his countrymen to victory in their struggle for independence.

CHAPTER III.

The Ohio Company Employ Christopher Gist to Explore the Lands Northwest of the Ohio River as Far West as the Great Falls — Gist Explores the Lands Between the Two Miamis, and on the Kentucky River.

In the meantime the Ohio Company had been making preparations to carry out their scheme of colonization, and employed Christopher Gist, of Virginia, a hardy pioneer, and noted hunter and woodsman, who had much experience in dealing with the Indians, to explore the country on the northwest of the Ohio River, as far west as the Falls of the Ohio, now Louisville,KY.

He started from Virginia on the 31st day of October, 1750, traveling through an unbroken wilderness over the mountains, and crossed the Ohio River near Beaver Creek, below Pittsburgh, and struck boldly out into the wilderness through the country now forming the great State of Ohio, examining it as he traveled, until he reached Muskingum, a town of the Wyandots and Mingoes, where he met George Croghan, the agent of the Governor of Pennsylvania.

Gist was well received by these tribes, as he was also by the Shawanees and Delawares, whom he visited with Croghan, at their town on the Scioto River. From the Shawanee town, at the mouth of the Scioto, Croghan and Gist traveled northwest near two hundred miles, crossing the Great Miama on a raft, swimming their horses, and arrived at the Indian town of Piqua, the principal town of the [Twigtwees], a tribe of the Miamis, on the 17th day of February, 1 75 1.

In this journey Gist had favorable opportunities for examining a wide extent of territory, which, on his return to Virginia, he described as incomparably fertile, covered with magnificent timber, watered by abundant creeks and rivulets, the forest and plains everywhere abounding in game and the streams with excellent fish, saying, "there was nothing wanting but cultivation to make it a delightful country."

From Piqua Gist and Croghan returned to the Shawnee town, on the Scioto, from whence Gist pursued his course toward the Great Falls of the Ohio, noting carefully the fitness of the country for cultivation, and the course and size of the streams emptying into the Ohio River.

It was at this time, between the 10th and 14th of March, 1751, he explored the country between the two Miamis, including the present site of Cincinnati, going up the Great Miami as far as Loramie Creek, forty six miles above the now city of Dayton, Ohio, and about one hundred miles above the mouth of that river.

The country in the neighborhood of Loramie Creek was the hunting ground of the Piankashas, another tribe of the Miamis. The English erected a fort and trading post on this creek the next year, 1752.

Gist had been warned by the Shawnees not to go to the Falls, as there was at that time a party of warriors, allies of the French, hunting in that vicinity; and that if he did, he would surely lose his scalp. Notwithstanding this warning, he came down the Miami, and proceeded toward his destination; but when within about fifteen or twenty miles of the Falls, he discovered unmistakable evidences of the proximity of savages, and seeing their traps and hearing the report of their guns, he changed his course, crossed the Ohio, and for six weeks followed up the Kentucky River, exploring the country bordering on its waters as far as Bluestone. This was nineteen years before Daniel and [his brother] Squire Boone visited the same country.

From Bluestone, Gist wended his weary way to Virginia, crossing the Kanawha River on a raft, reaching his home, on the Yadkin River, in May, only to find that the Indians had attacked the settlement and destroyed his house and property, but he soon learned that his family had escaped to a neighboring settlement and was safe.

It is possible, indeed highly probable, that French voyagers had navigated the Ohio River in its whole length in their canoes prior to this time. As they had several trading posts below the Great Falls, on its banks; but of this there is no authentic account, and at best is mere conjecture.

So far therefore, as is known, Christopher Gist was the first white man, either French, English, or American, who set foot upon, and explored, and published an account of the country between the two Miamis, in Hamilton County, OH, where John Cleves Symmes made his purchase in 1787, thirty-six years afterward, upon which Mathias Denman,

Robert Patterson and Israel Ludlow surveyed the next year, 1788, the town of Losantiville.

After Gist's return a report of his explorations was published in London in 1755, and in Philadelphia in 1756, which was the first authentic account given of the territory now composing the great State of Ohio, and created a great desire among colonists and emigrants to settle northwest of the Ohio, and especially in the Miami country.

Many efforts had been made by the colonists and English to establish settlements in the territory now comprising our great State after Gist's exploration, but all were unsuccessful. Thousands of pioneers had been murdered or captured and held prisoners. The borders of Pennsylvania and West Virginia had time and time again been almost totally depopulated by the tomahawk and scalping-knife of the ruthless and bloodthirsty savages, instigated, as was probably justly believed, by the French, to prevent the colonists or English from permanently occupying any part of the territory. And thus it continued until the breaking out of the Revolutionary War.

* * *

Here is an interesting YouTube film. A group of pioneers gather at Manasseh Cutler Church in Ipswich, Massachusetts to reenact the 1787 trip to the Northwest Territory to settle in the Ohio Country.

Go to YouTube and type: uxh92J4KIho

STANDARD OIL 1938 HISTORY OF THE SETTLEMENT OF OHIO PIONEERS OF THE OHIO COUNTRY DOCUMENTARY 47274

* * *

Hardships, trials and sufferings are sometimes, when we know it not, " blessings in disguise;" and in looking back over the early history of our country and realizing the blessings we now enjoy, he who does not see the hand of providence in all this must indeed be skeptical, for had the British Government been enabled to establish permanent settlements in the northwest with people loyal to the crown of Great Britain, and to have erected forts manned by British soldiers previous to the struggle for independence, with their navy and army attacking our country in the east and north and loyal subjects in the west, aided by the hordes of savages then occupying it, coming upon the rear, the patriots of '76 could never have achieved the independence of the colonies. And even after the independence of the colonies had been acknowledged, and the coveted territory had been ceded to the United States, there seemed to be a higher power than man preventing its occupation for some wise purpose. And not until the ordinance of 1787, making it an absolutely free territory where the clanking chains of slavery or involuntary servitude should never be heard, and establishing civil and religious liberty had been adopted as the fundamental law of the land, where every man could worship God according to the dictates of his own conscience; where there were none to molest or make them afraid; and declaring that religion, morality and education were necessary to the happiness of a free people — not until that had been adopted was there permitted any settlement to be made in our glorious State.

Appendix II

Extracts from Chapter 3, *The Ohio*

Richard Elwell Banta, 1949. Retrieved from https://archive.org.

Introduction
By D. B. McCoy.

In 1748, after the King George's War (the third of the four French and Indian Wars), Comte de la Galissoniere, the highest-ranking French official in North America, ordered Celeron de Bienville (also spelled Celeron de Blainville) to take 250 French soldiers to the Ohio Country to renew old friendships with local Native Americans and to drive the British traders from the region. Céloron de Bienville was a French military leader and explorer of Ohio in the mid-1700s.

Céloron carried out the mission in the summer of 1749. He made his way from Montreal by descending the Allegany River to the headwaters of the Ohio River (modern-day Pittsburgh), where he then proceeded down the Ohio. Céloron carried several lead plates with him. On these plates were pronouncements laying claim to the Ohio Country. Céloron Plate Transcription:

> "In the year of 1749, of the reign of Louis the 15th, King of France, we Céloron, commander of a detachment sent by Monsieur the Marquis de la Gallisonieré, Governor General of New

France, to reestablish tranquility in some Indian villages in these provinces, have buried this plate at the mouth of the River Chinodahichiltha on the 18th of August near the River Ohio, otherwise Beautiful River, as a monument of the renewal of the possession we have taken of the said River Ohio, and of all those which empty into it, and of all the lands on both sides as far as the sources of said rivers, as enjoyed or ought to have been enjoyed by the kings of France preceding, and as they have there maintained themselves by arms and by treaties, especially those of Ryswick, Utrecht, and Aix la Chapelle."

At the places where major rivers joined the Ohio, the party stopped and buried one of the tablets. On a nearby tree, a metal plaque was placed, asserting the claims of France and stating that the tablet lay nearby. This practice of burying plates first began in Europe in the Middle Ages and was a common way to show land ownership. In total, De Bienville is believed to have buried six plates.

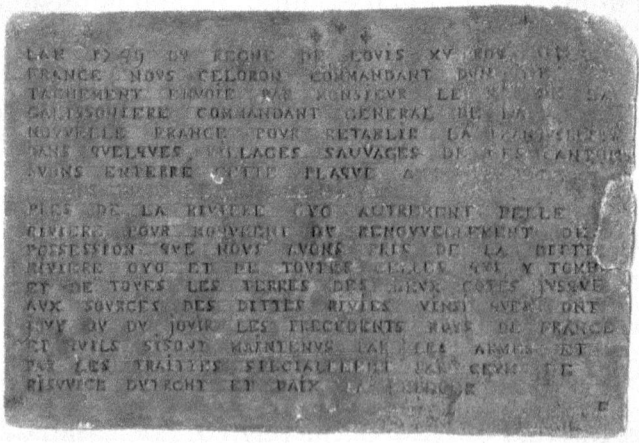

Only two have been found intact. (Don Pearce, Vice President of the Fort LeBoeuf Historical Society, 2021. YouTube video 8Fnd5m3TA9U.

Chapter 3: Someone Finds the OHIO - and France and England

The American partners in the Ohio Company of Virginia were quite well aware of the mode of procedure most likely to ensure success, if success was possible. They delegated a competent individual named Thomas Cresap to open a road from Cumberland, Maryland, to the Monongahela River. Though Cresap had no inkling of it, that road, after it had been considerably widened, would eventually be called Braddock's rather than Cresap's and would lead to the scene of a defeat bloody enough as a catastrophe to set a mark for persistently unadaptable British arms to shoot at for generations to come. The company also ordered a warehouse constructed on the site of Cumberland, Maryland, then on the far frontier. It also selected surveyor Christopher Gist as its agent to explore the upper Ohio and to locate the lands most eligible for its purposes.

By his agreement Gist was to receive a fee of £150 "and such further handsome allowance as his service should deserve." He was instructed to explore the Ohio as far as the Falls with particular instructions for securing the best possible lands for the company:

You are to go as soon as possible to the Westward of the Great Mountains ... to Search out and discover Lands upon the river Ohio. . . . When you find a large quantity of good, level Land, such as you think will suit the Company, You are to measure the Breadth of it, in three or four different Places, & take the Courses of the River & Mountains on which it binds in Order to judge the Quantity: You are to fix the Beginning &

Bounds in such a Manner that they may be easily found again ... the nearer in the Land lies, the better, provided it be good & level, but we had rather go quite down the Mississippi than take mean broken Land....

In addition to these positive instructions from the partners, Governor Robert Dinwiddie of Virginia privately commissioned Gist to talk with any Indians he might encounter and to invite them to a treaty meeting to be held at Logstown in 1752. Christopher Gist's substance was vouched for by this confidential mission as well as by the £150 fee — no small sum in those days, regardless of what "further handsome allowance" he might merit.

The total force that made up Gist's "expedition" consisted of himself and one young Negro slave, in contrast to Céloron's two hundred and twenty-two men. This ratio was typical of the frequently neglectful attitude toward the rich American hinterland that Englishmen exhibited: it resulted, twenty-five years later, in the loss of the lands by Britain, not to France but to her own neglected people.

Christopher Gist was the first officially accredited agent of Virginia known to have carefully explored and reported upon the upper Ohio. (He was indeed the first to report, but as for exploring there is in truth no telling but that some eighteenth-century Virginia prototype of Lawrence of Arabia may not have poked about the country in Shawnee garb long before the Ohio Company was organized.)

Born in Maryland, Gist had, judging by his journal, received a reasonably good English education. He had studied surveying, had acquired some property, and at the time of his selection as agent for the Ohio Company of Virginia was living near the home of Daniel Boone on the Yadkin River in upper North Carolina.

Gist left the company's warehouse at Cumberland and followed the road Cresap had blazed to the Forks of the Ohio. His journal began in October, 1750, and the early portion gave an excellent technical description of this trace. He found the land "mean, Stony and broken" to the Forks — as, indeed, it appears to the eye of the casual traveler today.

From the Forks he passed down the Ohio to Logstown. At that Shawnee-Mingo town, where a trading post had been established two years before and where Céloron had been offended by the British flag, he found a "Parcel of reprobate Traders." Probably there was nothing incontinent about the expletive; traders, certainly traders' employees such as these, were frequently of an order to make the term "reprobate" smack rather of flattery. Except for some of the owners of the posts and stocks, and an occasional young man who took employment temporarily for the purpose of learning the business and acquiring a foothold in the West, most traders were refugees from former haunts grown too hot for comfort or were men whose distaste for the restraints of civilization exceeded even that of the Indians. They were mainly a loose, dissolute, depraved lot and nothing is to be gained at this late date by gilding their sinful memories.

The traders at Logstown, despite their laxity of moral fiber, had a news item of importance both to Christopher Gist and to the cause of Virginian colonial sovereignty of the upper river; they reported that "George Croghan & Andrew Montour who were sent upon an Embassy from Pennsylvania to the Indians, were passed about a week before. . . ." Therein lies a story.

Both Pennsylvania and Virginia made fairly reasonable claims to the headwaters of the Ohio under the terms of their charters. Under certain stipulations of the original description, the western border of Pennsylvania was supposed to take the same curves as the Delaware River — obviously a difficult surveying assignment to be carried out in the trackless wilds. Hitherto there had been no call for a showdown on the matter; the country was not settled, and, since Virginians had engaged mainly in agriculture and had left Pennsylvanians to their comfortable Quaker mercantile pursuits, there was little competition for trade. Now, however, with the activities of the Ohio Company of Virginia obviously aggressive, the governor of Pennsylvania considered action expedient.

The very difference in the economies of the two colonies made Pennsylvania's interests more in accord with those of the Indians than were Virginia's. The Ohio Company of Virginia planned to colonize, to develop lands, and to farm, with trade only a secondary aim — the policy that the Indians had seen as fatal to themselves since settlement began — while Pennsylvania hoped only to retain control, to protect her licensed trade, and to maintain the Indians in their hunting grounds. Certainly the fur trade could not flourish in a land of cornfields and tobacco patches.

Even aside from considerations of this practical nature, however, Pennsylvania appeared to wish to continue the policy of keeping faith with the Indians which William Penn had inaugurated in the preceding century. Only the year before, in 1749, at the very time the British government was granting Indian lands to the Ohio Company of Virginia, Pennsylvania had taken stern action against a group of her own citizens who had encroached upon Indian rights. Several families had settled on Sherman's Creek (present Perry County, PA) and on complaint of the Indians the government had burned their cabins and moved the squatters back to the Susquehanna, above present Harrisburg.

One of the returned offenders celebrated the building of his new home on the Susquehanna with a housewarming festival which achieved such a degree of merriment that the host was accidentally shot by an Indian guest called "The Fish"; and The Fish was in turn killed by John Turner, a lodger with the family who soon after married the bereaved widow. The host, though mourned but briefly, left four sons behind to carry on his name. Two of them, Simon and George Girty, achieved an eminence of infamy as cruel renegades that has conferred on them an evil immortality.

Christopher Gist hoped that the Pennsylvania traders at Logstown would not realize his true mission for fear they would stop him. He was allowed to pass on, however, and at Beaver Creek he met one of the few traders as yet employed by the Ohio Company and together they went to the mouth of Muskingum River (present Marietta, Ohio). *En route* Gist commented upon the scarcity of good farm lands.

At the Wyandot town located near the junction of the Muskingum with the Ohio a certain George Croghan, recently appointed agent for the colony of Pennsylvania, had located one of his principal trading posts and Gist, noting the "English Colours hoisted on the [Wyandot] King's House, and at George Croghan's," decided to wait there for the arrival of the owner.

Now, Pennsylvania had chosen its agent as wisely, for its purpose, as had Virginia. Few educated men in America knew the Indians better and few were more respected by them. George Croghan, a literate Irishman, had come to America in 1741 as a lieutenant to Sir William Johnson, Indian agent of New York. He had left the service to set himself up as a trader, had been licensed by Pennsylvania in 1744, and had married a Mohawk woman, daughter of Nichos, a man prominent in the affairs of the Iroquois League.

Croghan's talents were soon recognized by both the Iroquois tribes and the colony of Pennsylvania; in 1746 he was made a counselor of the League and in 1749 he was appointed a justice of Cumberland County. He retained the confidence of the Indians on the Ohio and its tributaries throughout his life. Waiting at George Croghan's post at the Wyandot town, Christopher Gist was told by Croghan's five men that Croghan himself had missed a meeting with Céloron's expedition of the preceding year by only a fortunate few days, and that

Céloron had specifically ordered them to withdraw. Only recently, they said, the French had captured several English traders on the Ohio and had carried them and their "seven horseloads of Skins to a new Fort that the French were building on one of the branches of Lake Erie." Presently Croghan and Andrew Montour arrived.

This Andrew Montour was a character of stature equal to that of either Gist or Croghan. Son of Louis Couc Montour and his Indian wife, Madeleine — called always simply Madame Montour — and related to those other fabulous French-Indian Montours, Queen Esther, Queen Catharine, French Margaret, he and his family deserve a volume of their own; failing that, it must suffice to say that Andrew Montour was as important to the early opening of the Ohio Valley as any man.

Gist told Croghan of "my Business with the Indians [although not, one assumes, of the part of it relating to the aspirations of the Ohio Company of Virginia to the ownership of lands "good and level" on the north side of the Ohio River] and talked much of a Regulation of Trade with which they were much pleased, and treated Me very kindly."

On Christmas Day Gist "intended to read Prayers, but after inviting some of the White Men, they informed each other of my Intentions, and being of several different Persuasions, and few of them inclined to hear any Good, they refused to come." Sectarianism was already rearing its head on the Ohio! However, "one Thomas Burney a Black Smith who is settled there went about and talked to them, & several of them came, and Andrew Montour invited some well disposed Indians, who came freely...."

Gist read "The Doctrine of the Salvation Faith ... from the Homilies of the Church of England ... in the best manner" he could summon. He had, unwittingly, performed what must have been the first Protestant service on the Ohio or, indeed, in any part of what would become the Territory North-West of the River Ohio!

Apparently impressed, the Indians asked him to settle among them and to teach and baptize them — one trusts that Gist suffered a twinge of conscience at this — and even told him that he might build a fort to defend himself and them from the French. Gist declined, saying that his duties were to his governor.

Gist stayed at the Muskingum until January 15. Almost every day reports, came in of the troubles between the British traders and their partisans with the French and the Indians attached to French interests. Leaving the Muskingum he traveled down the north bank of the Ohio, describing the country and the small Indian towns — two, five, ten, twenty families — he encountered along that way. He was now accompanied by Croghan and Montour.

At Windaughalah's Delaware town "of about twenty families" on the "S. E. Side of Sciodoe Creek" [Scioto River] a council was called; Montour repeated a message from the Governor of Pennsylvania warning the Indians against the French, and invited them to the council at Logstown. "This," reported Gist, "is the last

Town of the Delawares to the Westward — The Delaware Indians by the best Accounts I could gather Consist of about 500 fighting Men all firmly attached to the English Interest, they are not properly a Part of the six Nations [the Iroquois League] but are scattered about amongst most of the Indians of the Ohio...."

Gist, Croghan, and Montour then moved down the Scioto to the Lower Shawnee Town, Chillicothe, and Gist recorded their experiences in his journal. It should be noted that this document, already quoted, is of particular interest because Gist was making an effort to give a detailed and lucid account of Indian life for the benefit of the generality of partners in the Ohio Company of Virginia. The British investors certainly, and many of those of Tidewater Virginia probably, were as ignorant of the minutiae of Indian life as most of us are today. Gist tried to give these men the whole picture of this country they soon hoped to claim: in doing so he did an invaluable service to history.

The party arrived opposite the town *and Here we fired our Guns to alarm the Traders, who soon answered, and came and ferryed Us over to the Town — The Land about the Mouth of Sciodoe Creek is rich but broken, fine Bottoms upon the River & Creek — The Shannoah [Shawnee] Town is situate upon both Sides the River Ohio, just below the Mouth of Sciodoe Creek and contains about 300 Men; there are about 40 Houses on the S. Side of the River and about 100 on the N. Side, with a kind of State-House of about 90 Feet long, with a light Cover of Bark, in which they hold their Councils — The Shanaws are not a Part of the Six Nations but were formerly at Veriance with* them, tho now reconciled; they are great Friends of the English, who once protected them from the Fury of the Six Nations, which they gratefully remember.

The party remained at this town, one of the most important Indian towns located immediately on the Ohio River in historic times, from January 31 to February 11, 1751. Gist took interesting notes:

While I was there the Indians had a very extraordinary kind of a Festival, at which I was present.... In the Evening a proper Officer made a public Proclamation that all the Indians' marriages were dissolved, and a Public Feast was to be held for three succeeding days after, in which the women, as their custom was, were again to choose husbands.

The next Morning, early, the Indians breakfasted, and after spent the Day in dancing till the Evening, when a plentiful Feast was pre- pared; after feasting, they spent the Night in dancing. The same way they spent the next two days till Evening, the Men dancing by themselves, and then the women in turns around the Fires, and dancing in their Manner in the Form of the Figure 8, about 60 or 70 at a time. The women, the whole Time they danced, sung a Song in their Language, the Chorus of which was,

*"I am not afraid of my Husband,
I will choose what Man I please."
(singing these lines alternately).*

The third Day in the Evening, the Men being about 100 in Number, [danced] some time at length, at other

Times in a Figure 8, quite round the Fort and in and out of the long House, where they held their Councils, the Women standing together as the Men danced by them; And as any of the Women liked a Man passing by, she stepped in and joined in the Dance, taking hold of the Man's Stroud whom she chose, and then continued in the Dance till the rest of the women stepped in and made their choice in the same manner; after which the dance ended, and they all retired to consummate.

Now Gist and Croghan made a sharp detour overland to the north, crossing the headwaters of those Ohio tributaries the Little and Great Miami and even approached the source of the Wabash, 150 miles or so north of the Ohio. Here they were away from Iroquois influence and in the land of the Miamis (or Twightwees, as Gist and other Englishmen called them). The Miamis had once suffered a terrific defeat at the hands of the Iroquois on the bluffs of the Wabash above Terre Haute, in present Indiana, but had now again grown strong and independent.

They had, since La Salle's day, been a loose association or confederacy which consisted of the Miami proper, possibly an eastern branch called Pickawillanies or Pickwaylinese (so called, perhaps, only by the British, who had a talent for misinterpreting Indian names) and certainly the Piankishaws, Kickapoos and Weas or Ouiatenons, according to the accepted French version of the name. These tribes appear to have been by no means definitely established as to division. It is not unlikely that a band called the "Pickwaylinese" when on the Pickaway Plains or in the neighborhood of Piqua (now a prosperous little Ohio city) might become known to whites as the "Eel River Miamis" when it chose to move to that tributary of the Wabash.

At any rate the Miami Confederacy was of considerable importance and Gist and Croghan gave its representatives the same softening words from their respective governors: "fear the French; trust the British and come to the council at Logstown for talk and gifts." The Miamis, even though they had been long-time friends of the French, appeared agreeable to the suggestion; meanwhile Gist noted the great eligibility of their lands to white settlement.

After a few days Gist, Croghan, and their party left, and presently Gist and his slave parted from the other two and followed the Little Miami back toward the Ohio. He reached the "Shannoah town" which he and Croghan had passed before; revealed to the inhabitants the friendly spirit of the Miamis and was tendered an "Entertainment in Honour of the late Peace with the Western Indians." Here he met one of the Mingo chiefs, who had "been down to the Falls of the Ohio" and "informed him of the King's Present, and the Invitation down to Virginia" (not, it will be noted, to Logstown, on the north shore of the Ohio, as had been the case when George Croghan was within hearing!). Three days later he crossed the Ohio and started downstream along the rough south bank.

Eighteen miles on the way "I Met two Men belonging to Robert Smith at whose House I lodged on this Side the Miamee River, and one Hugh Crawford, the said Robert Smith had given Me an Order upon these Men, for Two of the Teeth of a large Beast, which they were bringing from the Falls of the Ohio, one of which I brought in and delivered to the Ohio Company — Robert Smith informed Me that about seven Years ago these Teeth and Bones of three large Beasts (one of which was somewhat smaller than the other two) were found in a Salt Lick or Spring upon a small Creek which runs into the S. Side of the Ohio about 15 M. below the Mouth of the great Miamee River, and 20 above the Falls — He assured me that the Rib Bones of the largest of these Beasts were eleven Feet long, and the Skull Bone six Feet wide, across the Forehead, & the other Bones in Proportion; and that there were several Teeth there, some of which he called Horns, and said they were upwards of five Feet long, and as much as a Man could well carry; that he had hid one in a Branch at some Distance from the Place, lest the French Indians should carry it away — The Tooth which I brought in for the Ohio Company was a Jaw Tooth of better than four Pounds Weight...." This is the first British-American report on the Big Bone Lick of Kentucky.

For four days Gist continued along the south bank of the Ohio — seeing little, as he would today, of eligible farm land. He reached the mouth of the Licking River, but here he began to see the fresh tracks and newly set traps and to hear the gunfire of Indians; naturally he feared they were "French Indians," who, he had been warned, were hunting near by. With some misgivings as to the Ohio Company's satisfaction with his course, Gist decided to rely upon the reports he had had as to the configuration of the Falls — that they were "not very steep, on the S E Side there is a Bar of Land at some

Distance from the Shore, the Water between the Bar and the Shore is not above 3 feet deep, and the stream moderately strong" — and to go south across country to a pass which would soon take him safely out of reach of "French Indians" and back to Virginia.

Shortly after their tours, word of Gist and Croghan's movements reached New France and within a year the French began to assemble stores at Presque Isle, at present Erie, Pennsylvania, and to open a line of communication — with some rudimentary Fortifications — on the path to and down the Allegheny River toward the Forks of the Ohio. Their next aim was the construction of a fort at that point; a project to which the Ohio Company of Virginia was already committed. Those two conflicting plans were bound to cause trouble soon.

Appendix III

CHRISTOPHER GIST TIMELINE

+ 1682: Christopher and Edith arrived from England and settled on the south side of the Patapsco River in Baltimore County, Maryland

+ 1684: Father, Richard Gist, was born

+ 1705: Christopher Gist was born

+ 1730(?): Served as a Maryland Ranger

+ 1734: Received an appointment as overseer of the roads in Maryland

+ 1742: Entered mercantile business

+ 1743: Commissioned as coroner of Baltimore County

+ November 1745: Mounting debts forced Gist to move to a farm on the Yadkin River

+ 1757: Ohio Company of Virginia chartered

+ 1750: Hired by the Ohio Company of Virginia

+ September 11, 1750—May 19, 1751: First trans-Appalachian trip

+ November 4, 1751—March 29, 1752: Second trans-Appalachian trip

+ April 28, 1752: Named as a Company agent to the forthcoming Logstown Conference

+ June 1752: Represented the Ohio Company at the Logstown Conference

+ 1752, Fall: Built the settlement for the Ohio Company between the Youghiogheny River and Monongahela Rivers referred to as "Gist's Plantation," "Gist's Settlement," and "Gist's."

+ July 25, 1753: Gist obtained a surveyor's commission from the College of William and Mary.

+ August 17, 1753: Appointed one of the Justices of Augusta County, Virginia (at the time the plantation was a part of Augusta County, VA)

+ November 17, 1753—January 2, 1754: Accompanied George Washington to Fort LeBoeuf

+ July 5, 1754: French destroyed Gist's Plantation

+ May 1755: Appointed head guide to British and Colonial forces by General Braddock

+ October 1, 1755: Commissioned lieutenant in Virginia Regiment

+ October 10, 1755: Received word of his new commission as Captain of a Company of Scouts

+ July 25, 1757: Appointed Deputy Agent of Indian Affairs for the Southern Department

+ July 25, 1759: Christopher Gist died while escorting a party of Catawba Indians between Williamsburg and Winchester at the age of fifty-four

SOURCES

Emerson's magazine and Putnam's monthly, Volume 5, NO 40, 1857.

Lynch, Bradford Gist. "Christopher Gist," *The Times, Westminster*, MD. Nov 18, 1932.

ORRILL, LAWRENCE A. "CHRISTOPHER GIST AND HIS SONS." Western Pennsylvania Historical Magazine, Volume 15, Number 3, August 1932.

Swetnam, George. *The Many Hats of Christopher Gist.* The Pittsburgh Press - Mar 18, 1973. This can be found on the internet.

     *   *   *

Bailey, Kenneth P. *Christopher Gist: Colonial frontiersman, explorer, and Indian agent.* Archon Books (1976).

Bailey, Kenneth P. *THE OHIO COMPANY OF VIRGINIA AND THE WESTWARD MOVEMENT 1748-1792* . ARTHUR H. CLARK COMPANY (1939). http://archive.org/details/ohiocompanyofvirbail

Banta, Richard Elwell, *The Ohio*. University Press of Kentucky (1998).

Dorsey, Jean Muir and Maxwell Jay Dorsey. *Christopher Gist of Maryland and Some of His Descendants, 1679-1957.* John S. Swift Co. (1958).

Gist, Christopher. *Christopher Gist's Journals With Historical, Geographical And Ethnological Notes And Biographies Of His Contemporaries edited* by William M. Darlington. Forgotten Books (August 23, 2012).

Jones, Adolphus Eberhardt, Extracts from the history of Cincinnati and the territory of Ohio, 1888. Retrieved from https://archive.org.

Johnson, Charles A. CHAPTER XIV "Captain Christopher Gist," Wise County, Virginia. (1938.) Overmountain Press (1988).

Misencik, Paul R. and Sally E. Misencik. *With George Washington in the Wilderness: The Frontier Life of Christopher Gist* (2022).

Powell, Allan. *Christopher Gist, Frontier Scout*. Burd Street Press (1992).

Truman, Timothy. *Straight Up to See the Sky*. Eclipse Books (April 1992).

Washington, George. "From George Washington to John Robinson, 30 May 1757" [RE Christopher Gist]. https://founders.archives.gov/documents/Washington/02-04-02-0099

Wig, Christian. *Annosanah: A Novel Based on the Life of Christopher Gist*. Heritage Books, Inc., (2004).

Wilson, James Grantand and John Fiske, *Appleton's Cyclopedia of American Biography* Vol. 2, 1887.

David B. McCoy earned his history teaching degree from Ashland University and his graduate degree from Kent State University. After teaching thirty-two years, David retired to write short books on a wide variety of topics.

Short, concise, and informative, most Spare Change Press ® publications are generally less than 100 pages.

www.amazon.com/author/davidmccoy

David will appear as the on-camera expert on the Christopher Gist episode of *Into The Wild Frontier* series sometime late 2022 or 2023.

For a preview of the *Into the Wild Frontier* series

type in the YouTube search box

UQLCxGZfYEw

www.ingramcontent.com/pod-product-compliance
Lightning Source LLC
Chambersburg PA
CBHW070510100426
42743CB00010B/1798